DANCING
LESSONS

DANCING LESSONS

How I Found Passion and Potential on the Dance Floor and in Life

CHERYL BURKE

WILEY

John Wiley & Sons, Inc.

Published by John Wiley & Sons, Inc., Hoboken, New Jersey
Published simultaneously in Canada

Design by Forty-five Degree Design LLC

Photo insert credits: Pages 2, 3, 4, 5, 6, 8, 9 (top), 12 (bottom), 14, courtesy of author; page 7, courtesy of Burke family; pages 9 (bottom), 10, 11, A. Wolfe; page 12 (top), Jack Ketsoyan; page 13, courtesy of Jazzercise, Inc.; page 15, courtesy Forever Tango/Luis Bravo Productions; page 16, copyright BBC Worldwide, photo by Adam Larkey

For general information about our other products and services, please contact our Customer Care Department within the United States at (800) 762-2974, outside the United States at (317) 572-3993 or fax (317) 572-4002.

Wiley also publishes its books in a variety of electronic formats. Some content that appears in print may not be available in electronic books. For more information about Wiley products, visit our web site at www.wiley.com.

Library of Congress Cataloging-in-Publication Data:

Burke, Cheryl.
  Dancing lessons : how I found passion and potential on the dance floor and in life / Cheryl Burke.
    p. cm.
  ISBN 978-0-470-64000-5 (cloth); ISBN 978-0-470-95135-4 (ebk);
  ISBN 978-0-470-95137-8 (ebk); ISBN 978-0-470-95138-5 (ebk)
    1. Burke, Cheryl. 2. Dancers—United States—Biography. 3. Choreographers—United States—Biography. 4. Ballroom dancing. 5. Dancing with the stars (Television program) I. Title.
  GV1785.B86A3 2011
  792.8028092—dc22
  [B]   2010042164

Printed in the United States of America

10 9 8 7 6 5 4 3 2 1

CONTENTS

CONTENTS

FOREWORD

by Tom Bergeron

When Cheryl asked me to write the foreword for her book, eventually I was flattered. Why "eventually"? I'm not proud to admit this, but before I arrived at "flattered" I had to work through another emotion: jealousy. After all, I was fifty-three years old before I published my first book, *I'm Hosting as Fast as I Can!* (available at Amazon.com and bargain bins everywhere). Cheryl is only twenty-six! That's less than half of my age (as she is always fond of pointing out to me). How is that even remotely fair?

I'll grant you that Cheryl is ridiculously talented, absolutely gorgeous, and a genuinely warm and wonderful person. I'll even admit that in addition to being my friend, she's been one of my favorite dancers from the moment she joined the *Dancing with the Stars* cast in season two. But this published-author business was going too far! Couldn't she at least wait until she turned thirty? Why don't you blog for a while first, Cheryl? Twitter your little heart out. Do you have to write a whole book? It makes me look like a middle-aged (okay, advanced middle-aged) slacker. Heck, when I was twenty-six I was still waiting for my skin to clear up!

Even with sequins and a spray tan, jealousy isn't pretty. And for me it was only a passing phase. The green-eyed monster finally released its grip, because in the end I realized that I'd want to read this book. Cheryl has fascinated me since the first time I watched her dance. If you're a fan of *Dancing with the Stars*, I'm betting you feel the same. Who wouldn't want a chance to get to know her better?

When season two of *Dancing with the Stars* began in early 2006, I was uneasy. Our debut season, the previous year, had consisted of only six one-hour episodes and had been a smash hit. A special that aired a few months later, *Dancing with the Stars Dance-Off*, hadn't fared as well in the ratings. I was concerned that the bloom was already fading from our newborn rose.

I needn't have worried. When season two premiered, the audience came back and then got bigger. One of the reasons for that was the arrival of a charismatic professional dancer named Cheryl Burke. Teamed with pop star Drew Lachey, Cheryl quickly became the pro to watch. She went on to win the coveted mirror ball trophy with Drew in season two, and she won it again when she was teamed with football great Emmitt Smith in season three. Cheryl wasn't just dancing with stars, she was becoming one herself.

I don't think anything can prepare you for being recognized almost anywhere you go. I'd worked in radio and television for more than thirty years before coming to *Dancing with the Stars*, eleven of them on a national level, and the heightened profile we suddenly enjoyed knocked even me for a loop. But I got off easy. For a young woman suddenly thrust into the media spotlight, the scrutiny of the tabloid press can be relentless and downright cruel. Cheryl certainly endured her share of it. In March 2009, when *TV Guide* featured her standing triumphantly (and stunningly) on its cover with the headline "Cheryl Gets Fierce!" she proved she was more than up to the challenge.

But it goes deeper than that. In navigating through some rough waters and coming to terms with both the price and the privilege of fame, Cheryl emerged different—happier, I think, and also clearer about who she is and where she wants to go. That's quite an accomplishment when you're only twenty-six. It's actually quite an accomplishment even if you're seventy-six. A lot of people go through their entire lives wrestling with those questions without ever coming close to the answers.

Once I agreed to write this foreword, Cheryl admitted to me that she was nervous about what I'd write. I can understand why, I suppose. Our friendship has taken on aspects of a surrogate father-daughter relationship: relentless teasing leavened with occasional heart-to-heart talks. It's not unusual, seconds before going live in front of an audience of twenty million people, for me to stroll over to Cheryl as she prepares for a complicated dance number and tell her, "Don't screw up this time!" During a show for which she was wearing a dress of a billowy silver material, I waited for her to stand at my side with her partner before asking the television audience, "Is anybody missing a weather balloon?"

She gets really nervous when I *don't* tease her. For a whole day, during both the dress rehearsal and the live broadcast, I effusively and honestly complimented her dress, her hair, and her overall look. She kept waiting for a zinger; it never came. By the end of the day she implored me, "Don't ever do that again!" Given that attitude, she must be a wreck since reading that I think she's "ridiculously talented, absolutely gorgeous, and a genuinely warm and wonderful person." Too bad, Cheryl. Deal with it.

Sit back, keep reading, and see if you don't agree with me.

ACKNOWLEDGMENTS

This book would not have been possible without the help and support of many wonderful people in my life.

Monica Rizzo, thank you not only for writing this book with me but also for being equal parts therapist, confidante, and cheerleader along the way.

Holly Root at Waxman Agency and Christel Winkler and the team at John Wiley & Sons, thank you all for believing in my story.

Tiffany Yecke Brooks, you made all of our lives easier when you came on board.

Susan Madore, you have been in my corner from the start. I don't know what I'd do without you.

A big thank you to my entire *Dancing with the Stars* family—
you know who you are. Andrea Wong, Izzie Pick, Deena Katz,
and Conrad Green, thank you a million times over for casting
me! Rob Wade and the entire production team, Tom Bergeron,
all of my fellow pro dancers, and all of my wonderful celebrity
partners over the years, it's been the experience of a lifetime,
and I love you all.

Yuki Saegusa, thank you for making my dreams become a
reality.

Allan Tornsberg, thank you for being the best dance coach
and mentor a person could ever have. Most of all, thank you
for believing in me. I will always look up to you.

Wendy Johnson, thank you for your inspiration and for
telling me that I could do *Dancing with the Stars* when I was so
unsure in the beginning.

Joanne McCarthy, "guardian angel," thank you for being
my rock and the best friend I never had. Love ya, girl!

Jack Ketsoyan, thank you for being such a great listener and
friend to me.

Sheila Pacete, you always make me smile. You are such an
amazing person in my life.

Evan Hainey and Chad Christopher, thank you both for
everything.

To all of the fans who've told me that I've inspired them
to take up dance or try to live a healthier life, or who've simply
loved watching me dance every week on television, I thank you
from the bottom of my heart. Your enthusiasm, kindness, and

love are gifts that have lifted my spirits on many occasions. You mean more to me than you'll ever know.

Most of all, I want to extend my heartfelt gratitude to my family: my mother, Sherri Burke; my father, Stephen Burke; my stepfather, Robert Wolf; and my sisters, Mandy Wolf and Nicole Wolf. Your love and encouragement over the years have meant the world to me as I've pursued my passion. I am truly blessed.

INTRODUCTION

*I*f someone had told me four years ago that I'd be writing a book about my life, I would have flat-out exclaimed, "You're crazy!" I was a competitive ballroom dancer living in Harlem and struggling to make ends meet. If you had asked me whether I was happy with my life, I probably would have said that I was. After all, I was making a living doing what I loved. But if you had asked me if I had an interesting life, I would have had to say no.

Then one day I received a phone call offering me an interview with ABC for *Dancing with the Stars*. On that day, everything in my life as I knew it changed.

These days I'm known mostly for being a dancer on the highest-rated dance show on American television. But I'm also a clothing designer, a dance studio owner, and a businesswoman. Doors have opened up for me that I never imagined would be possible.

Four years ago I would have balked at the suggestion that I have something to say that anyone would want to hear. Now, however, dance hasn't just given me opportunities, it's also given me a public voice and a way to reach out to people.

I have a variety of life experiences to share with the people who have come to know me and embrace me as a dancer on *Dancing with the Stars*. Almost every day, people I've never met come up to me while I'm waiting at the airport, running errands, or grabbing coffee with friends. They tell me with enthusiasm and genuine gratitude that I have done amazing things to inspire them. Older people tell me that I have motivated them to dance again. Mothers tell me that their daughters want to learn how to dance just like me. And almost all of them tell me that when they watch the show, it makes them happy. Hearing these testimonies and knowing that I've influenced people in such a positive way gives me the most incredible feeling.

Dancing has been my passion since I was a young girl growing up in San Francisco. Throughout the years, it has also helped me to learn about all aspects of life. I'm now at a point in my life, both personally and professionally, at which I believe that by opening up and sharing my story I will be able to encourage others to believe in themselves and their dreams and the pursuit of their passions. There is a lot more to me than what people see on television. I've had my share of personal and professional challenges, but I did not let them defeat me. I want people to know that we all can overcome whatever life throws our way.

Dancing with the Stars premiered on ABC in 2005 and attracted enough viewers to encourage the network to put it back on the air as soon as possible in 2006. That's when I came into the picture—and when my life changed.

I really had no interest in being on television before that point. I was curious but not especially serious about it. In retrospect, I sure am glad that I went to that first interview. The show has reignited the country's interest in dancing, and I'm so grateful that I've been able to be part of it.

Because of my role on the program, I have met some of the most inspiring people and grown through some tremendously challenging circumstances. The doors that have opened for me because of *Dancing with the Stars* and the perspective I have gained completely changed the way I view my life, my art, and my reason for dancing. These opportunities have given me a new sense of strength and purpose that I believe can help to encourage other people to overcome the past, relate in new ways to the present, and reach for the future.

For some dancers, hitting their mid-twenties can signify a time for change. It's often an end to a career in ballet or ballroom dancing and the start of a soul-searching journey for what's next. I am happy to say that I am not in the midst of a quarter-life crisis, by any stretch of the imagination. In fact, I believe that I've just hit my stride, transitioning from being a ballroom dancer on a TV show to a person who symbolizes dance, fitness, and vitality. I own and operate two dance studios in California, and I'm currently working on franchising studios around the country. I also took on the role of fitness-wear designer when I launched my own clothing line for FitCouture.com in 2008.

I have learned so much about life and business through dance, and although my story is specific to me, the themes of dreaming bigger and trying harder are universal. I hope that by sharing my triumphs and struggles, I can inspire people to pursue the things in their lives that make them happy and keep them young. The fulfillment I feel in my life is not just in reference to my career; it has spilled over into my personal life. Over the years I have come to realize that I deserve more in life than I had been allowing myself to believe.

My perspectives on work, family, love, and self-acceptance will, I hope, speak to people of all ages. My experiences have taken me around the globe. They have made me smile, they have made me cry, and they have helped me to learn and grow and become the person I am today.

So here is my life story, which I'm telling through eight different dance styles that fans have seen me perform on television. Just like the various dances, my life has been full of emotion, joy, sadness, fantasy, and reality. But most important, it's been about pursuing my passion and striving to be the best dancer, the best daughter, the best businesswoman, and most of all, the best person I can be.

THE FREESTYLE

Finding Myself in the Spotlight

1

The freestyle dance is not restricted by any conventional steps or required choreography. It is simply a dance in which the dancer can showcase whatever movement or emotion seems appropriate.

I've always been kind of a play-by-the-rules girl; I tend to like things structured, predictable, and sometimes even a little boring. But all of that changed on February 26, 2006, the last night of my first season on *Dancing with the Stars*. It was an evening when all of my rules went out the window and everything in my life suddenly changed for the better. Yet I almost missed out on what has been the greatest adventure of my life so far because I was afraid to break out of the comfortable mold in which I was living. I know it sounds unbelievable to say that I almost turned down the opportunity to star as a professional dancer on the hit reality dance show, but that's the truth.

Six months prior to that February night, I was living in New York City with my boyfriend and ballroom dance partner when suddenly I received a phone call from one of the show's producers, who wanted to talk to me about the show on ABC. The dancer Louis van Amstel, whom I knew from the ballroom dance world, worked on season one of the show, and he recommended that the producers get in touch with me. I didn't have an agent at the time; some of the producers just saw me perform at a competition in Los Angeles and agreed that I might be exactly what they were looking for, so Louis passed along my number.

My immediate reaction was to turn them down because of my strong fear of cameras. But the more I thought about it, the more I figured, "Why not? Give it a chance, at least, before you turn them down." So I went to Manhattan for the meeting, but even then I was not bowled over with enthusiasm. I kind of downplayed it to my dancer friends, who were as skeptical as I was.

However, there was something in my gut that kept nagging me to jump at this opportunity—that I should just go for broke and see what happened. At the time, I was barely making ends meet as a competitive ballroom dancer and a dance instructor, so the prospect of a steady job—as steady as a job in television can be—as well as the prospect of going to sunny Los Angeles from snowy New York City in the middle of winter were an appealing combination. The show had been pretty popular in its first season, and my boyfriend and I were kind of on the outs anyway. Everything seemed to be pointing me in the direction of the show. What did I have to lose, really?

So I said yes, packed my bags, and jetted off to a city I was barely familiar with and in which I knew hardly a soul. I was very lucky, however, to have a firmly established support system set up through the show. Within just a few days of landing in Los Angeles, I met close to a hundred people: producers, hair and makeup artists, wardrobe people, photographers, and fellow ballroom dancers. My head wasn't just spinning, it was doing pirouettes.

I was partnered with the singer Drew Lachey of the popular group 98 Degrees. Drew and I complemented each other with our strengths. I was good at dancing and teaching dance, and he was a good student and a natural-born ham for the cameras. Week after week we learned our routines, got good scores from the judges, and received lots of votes from the fans. It was a lot of fun but overwhelming at times, too, as I skyrocketed from being "just a dancer" to "that girl on *Dancing with the Stars*."

I'd always heard "Be careful what you wish for, for you just might get it," but I never realized how true it was until Drew and I started advancing week after week. It's not that I didn't want the two of us to do well on the show, but every week that we moved further in the competition meant another round of interviews with the press. I was terrified of the cameras—beyond terrified. The fame was new to me, and the whole idea of talking to the press was the scariest thing I could imagine, because I've always been a very shy and private person.

I was nervous to be in front of cameras and have microphones shoved in my direction. It seems silly; after all, I make my living in front of millions of television viewers each week, so why should a one-to-one interview in front of a camera make me break out in a sweat? It's simple: I am at home when I'm on the dance floor. For that one minute and thirty seconds that I have to dance on live television, I'm good to go because I am in my element, in my own world. It's the days and hours leading up to that time, and the moments right after, that I'm on edge. But unfortunately, I had to take one with the other.

"You're the performer, Drew, so you're used to all of this attention. You do all the talking, okay?" I begged him.

"Cheryl, you're an amazing dancer," he scoffed. "People want to talk to you, too."

"No," I insisted. "You are the celebrity, not me. I'm the dancer. Let me do what I need to do on the dance floor. You can do all the talking."

Finally Drew agreed—kind of. "Okay, leave it to me. But if they ask you something, don't be afraid. Be yourself. You'll be fine." I prayed that he was right.

As the season went on, people kept asking me little things about myself: Where was I from? Was I really only twenty-one? How did I like all of this attention? For that last one, I just tried to think of a polite way to say, "I don't! You're scaring me to death!"

A few weeks before we actually made it to the season two finale (and in between all of those terrifying interviews), the producers asked us what song we wanted for our freestyle dance. They surveyed the remaining three couples, because the show's music clearance department needed time to license the songs so it could play them on the air.

The freestyle dance has become one of the most popular dances on the show in the past ten seasons (there are two seasons a year) because for the first time the couples don't have to adhere to the strict rules of the ballroom. This is a time in which the couples get to have fun, let loose, and unleash their creativity. Just about anything is acceptable. The number one rule is not to follow any rules.

Drew was practically salivating at the chance to dance a no-holds-barred routine to any song he wanted. I found him one day sitting in his dressing room poring over the iTunes catalog on his laptop.

"Cheryl, I found it. Let me play this for you," he said excitedly.

"Save a Horse (Ride a Cowboy)" by the country duo Big & Rich came pounding out of the speakers, and I just stared at Drew as though he were crazy. I had never heard the song before, I had never heard of Big & Rich, and I could not possibly imagine myself dancing to country music.

I wanted to have more of a Latin influence in our music and our routine, something that would feel more traditional and comfortable for the kind of partner dancing I was used to. But Drew was adamant that his country song would be great for our freestyle. He insisted that this was exactly what the producers meant when they said to let loose and do something original and completely unexpected. He had me there.

One of the producers happened to be in the hallway, and Drew summoned her into the room to tell her his idea. Of course, she absolutely loved it. I was outnumbered. So that night, I got myself a copy of the song and played it over and over to get it into my head and my body. The more I played it, the more the song grew on me, but when I tried to figure out how I would choreograph the routine, I was stumped.

If there's one thing that can get you in a different frame of mind, it's looking the part you want to play.

We went to the wardrobe department, and the staff had a field day with our song. The innuendo of the song helped them conjure up sexy cowboy and cowgirl costumes for Drew and me: Drew's costume was a sleeveless shirt and tight jeans, and mine was a tiny pair of denim shorts and a bra top. We both rocked cowboy hats and boots.

Even suited up, I was still panicking two days before the finale as I tried to put the finishing touches on the dance. Drew kept insisting, "We need to spice this up, Cheryl!" We'd been dancing together for weeks, and now that we actually had a dance to do with no rules, we both became choreographers—and he was a pretty ambitious one. He wanted to add more lifts, more playfulness with the movements to jibe with the flirtatiousness of the song. He kept saying, "This is good, but let's make it great. It's our last dance. Let's push it as far as we can—and then a little bit more."

Egging things along even more was Drew's wife, Lea—Drew's very pregnant and about-to-give-birth-at-any-minute wife, Lea. She came to the rehearsal to see how we were doing, and I was sure she'd cringe when she saw the routine. Instead she insisted that we add even more suggestive moves. She kept saying, "This is a sexy, suggestive song, and you guys have to really play off the lyrics more. Don't be afraid. Go for it!"

So we did. Drew and Lea both had great ideas and awesome enthusiasm. Drew had such a good gut instinct about the whole thing, and his wife's stamp of approval validated our efforts. Our goal was to have fun and have the audience have fun with us, and it looked as though we were on the right track.

As creative and fun as their ideas were, however, I was still having some doubts. On the one hand, I was feeling carefree. I knew that people were going to be talking about this dance the next day. On the other hand, I was a little nervous about *how* they would be talking about it. We were an eight o'clock, family-friendly show. What would viewers think when they saw me straddle Drew's back while he was in a push-up position and lift him up and down? I also began to worry that people would think we were cruel or insensitive for doing such a suggestive dance with Lea sitting in the front row. But it was too late to back out now.

Before we stepped out onto the stage, I got a pang in my belly. I always get the same pang right before I'm about to dance. It's just part of my preperformance routine. That night, though, it was much bigger than ever before.

We got the call to take our spots on the ballroom floor. The audience was going nuts. I could not hear a thing over the crazy thumping of my heartbeat. Drew was pumped. He jumped up and down a couple of times to warm up. I stood still and just tried to absorb it all. I am sure that I looked calm to the people in the audience, but inside I was about to explode. People were screaming our names, clapping, and cheering wildly—and we hadn't even started our dance yet. Drew looked over at me and smiled. He raised his eyebrows as if to say, "Here we go, girl." I think I smiled back at him. It may have been a grimace, actually. What were we about to do? Could we pull it off?

All of my fears and insecurities, the adrenaline rushing through my body, the perspiration on the palms of my hands— everything came to a boil. Then the music started, and like so many times before, the nervousness vanished. The one minute and thirty seconds that I had to dance was magic. That was the easy part. We tore through our routine and never missed a beat. The audience was on their feet, screaming and applauding throughout the routine. We were doing what we were told to do: go all out and just go crazy.

During the performance I was, of course, focused on the dance. But I did manage to catch a glimpse of the audience. Everyone was screaming, laughing, and clapping. I glanced over at the judges' table at one point, too, and I saw Bruno Tonioli out of the corner of my eye. He was banging his hand on the table, his mouth wide open in disbelief. Carrie Ann Inaba was laughing and smiling. Toward the end of the dance

I even stole a peek at Len Goodman, the gentleman judge of the ballroom world. I wondered if he'd think our performance was too over-the-top or suggestive for the program. It turned out that he had the biggest smile of all. These little glimpses at people as we were performing only pushed Drew and me into character more. We hammed it up.

At the end of the routine, when Drew hit the floor in a push-up position and I straddled his back, mimicking how a rodeo champ would ride a bucking bronco, the screams and cheers got louder. Our big finish was greeted with a raucous standing ovation. We both were out of breath, yet we were so jazzed by the audience response that we wanted to do the dance all over again. It reminded me why I was there: this is what I do best. I love to dance. I love to perform. I love to entertain. It was the beginning of a new adventure for me.

Always embrace new adventures.

Drew and I were declared the winners of season two on that cold night in February, when we brought some serious heat to the dance floor. Before that night I was more or less anonymous. I could eat, shop, walk, and work out anywhere I wanted to and at any time. People didn't know my name. I might look familiar, but they weren't quite sure where to place me, so they didn't say anything. That all changed on February 26, 2006.

Confetti dropped from the ceiling as the live orchestra played celebratory music. The crowd was cheering. My mom was crying. Within minutes cameras hovered around us.

DANCE TIP

No matter what dance you perform, you should have fun doing it—and don't ever fake it. When I dance, I don't put on any show faces. Facial expressions are an extension of the body's expressions and should come from somewhere special and authentic. When you feel the dance and the music, that, in turn, dictates how you will emote. People can tell if you're being artificial.

Reporters shoved tape recorders and microphones under our chins. I felt like the proverbial deer in the headlights. People were asking me all kinds of questions. How I did I feel being a winner? How was I going to celebrate? Where was I going to put my trophy? Would I be back next season?

Whoa—that last question stopped me in my tracks. Next season? It didn't even occur to me that I would be back on the show. It hadn't crossed my mind that the show would want to hire me for another round. That kind of job security just doesn't happen in the dance world. But that night, when Drew and I threw out the rule book and just went freestyle, it kicked off a new life for me. It was a new beginning, and I couldn't wait to get started.

THE CHA-CHA-CHA

My First Steps

The cha-cha-cha is a fast, upbeat dance—cheeky and flirtatious with lots of hip action. This Latin ballroom dance originates from Cuba and is a great first dance for novices who want to learn basic ballroom moves. Rumor has it that the name *cha-cha-cha* came about because of the sounds a dancer's shoes make when he or she takes the quick steps that are the core of the routine, but it is usually referred to by a shortened version of its name: the cha-cha. Another appealing aspect of the cha-cha is that it can be performed to all types of music, including pop, rock, and authentic and rhythmic Cuban music.

Sometimes just a little success can create the momentum you need to do incredible things. I have definitely found this to be true; sometimes the most unlikely dancers find themselves performing on a level they never would have thought possible just a few weeks before.

For the competing couples' first performance on *Dancing with the Stars*, it's very common to have them dance the cha-cha because of its simplicity and repetitive nature. It can also be performed to the beat of a lot of different types of music, which makes it very versatile.

Sometimes the simplest idea is the most ingenious.

In my nine seasons of *Dancing with the Stars*, I've danced with partners of all ages and all ability levels, but one of my most surprising experiences as a professional dancer on the show occurred when I got a call from Rob Wade, one of the show's producers, who teased me about who my partner would be on season nine.

"You've got an interesting one this season," Rob said coyly.

"Really? How interesting?" I asked.

"Incredibly interesting. People are going to be talking about this one the minute we announce his name."

My interest was piqued, to say the least. Maybe I was a little bit nervous. After all, *interesting* is a very vague description, so it was making my imagination run wild with the possibilities.

A couple of days later I was informed that my partner would be Tom DeLay, the former majority leader of the House of Representatives. I must admit that I do not closely follow politics, so I did what I've done with practically all of my partners. I went to my computer and Googled his name in order to get all the details. The first thing I clicked on was a news article about conspiracy and money-laundering charges that were brought against him in 2005. There was also a picture of him—his mug shot. He pleaded not guilty, claiming it was all just a political move to smear his reputation, and the case never even made it to court (in fact, the charges were eventually dropped in August 2010), but I was completely confused.

"What on earth?" I muttered to myself as I read about his colorful history as a politician. The more I read, the more I was surprised and wondered, "Why would he want to be on *Dancing with the Stars?*"

I was baffled, but I was also intrigued. I will probably never understand how the producers arrive at the partners they assign to me each season, but one thing is for sure: every person I've been paired with has been an incredible human being, and it turned out that Tom was no exception. When I first started reading about Tom, I took what I read with a grain of salt. I knew that we would be able to work things out as long as we communicated with each other and as long as he was willing to try his best and be open with everything I wanted to show him.

At our first meeting, Tom and I talked about his experience as a dancer. He had always enjoyed dancing socially; he and his wife, Christine, often went line dancing, and he said he loved to move to live music. But he had never had any formal training, and he was hoping that the *Dancing* experience would teach him some different dances he could enjoy with his wife. He was a fan of the show and thought it would be fun for American audiences to see a different side of his personality. He was so incredibly enthusiastic about everything from the start that it was impossible not to like him.

At our first rehearsal, we stood in front of the mirrors in the dance studio. I started showing him the basic steps to the cha-cha. I started counting "two, three, cha-cha-cha." (Counting for dance starts with two.) I like to have my partners dance without music at first just to see how quickly they pick up the steps. I think it's necessary to take baby steps in order to determine what people can and can't do; then I know how to build a routine around their strengths. Some people get it right away, whereas others take a bit of time.

Within about ten seconds of doing the basic cha-cha moves, Tom asked eagerly, "What about the music?"

"No music yet," I explained to him. "I want to get a sense of how you move and how you follow directions. This way I can see what kind of rhythm you have, and then I will put on the music."

"Oh, I really think we need the music now," he pleaded with me. He was clearly excited about jumping right into the routine.

I laughed and told him that I wanted to go through the steps a few more times, and then we'd put on the music. But when we did, there was a problem. The song Tom and I were assigned was the 1960s classic "Wild Thing," by the Troggs, because the producers thought it would be fun to play off Tom as a conservative Republican with a strait-laced public image. But he thought otherwise.

"Oh, I can't dance to that song. No, no," Tom said to me, shaking his head. "We have to find another song."

"But this will be fun," I told him.

"No, no, not to this song, darlin'," he replied politely and a little apologetically. "I'd feel better if we had something more traditional."

I called Joe Sungkur, our supervising producer, on the phone to see about getting another song, but he didn't want to change it.

"This song is perfect for the show," Joe said. "You have to convince him of that, Cheryl. We really need you to do this."

"But he really doesn't want to do this, and I can understand his point of view," I argued.

"That's fine, but we have a television show, and our purpose is to entertain the audience," Joe insisted. "We really want this song on the show. Try to convince him to do it."

We ended the phone call, and I took a deep breath. Obviously, Tom wanted a more conventional, classic cha-cha, but the show does not trend toward classic, authentic music. In fact, the show is famous for pairing nontraditional music with the dances. I explained to Tom that Joe wanted us to stick with the song. I promised him it would be a hit with the fans, if he'd just give it a chance. He gave me the ultimate compliment.

"Well, you are the expert entertainer here, not me," he said. "If you say we need to do this, then I trust your decision."

Wow. I took a deep breath. I was flattered that he trusted and respected me.

We hit another potential snag two days before our wardrobe fitting for the season's first show when Tom's daughter, Dani, laid out some ground rules for me.

"My dad will not want to wear rhinestones," Dani said to me firmly. "He will eventually have to go back to Washington."

"That's what they all say," I retorted, laughing.

"No, I'm serious," Dani said.

"Me, too," I replied.

The truth is that nobody ever jumps in with both feet when coming on *Dancing with the Stars*. Everyone dips a toe in the water first. None of the guys wants to wear the tight pants or the low-cut shirt. For Tom, it was all about not having him look too flashy, and that was fine. But I knew that he needed flair. After all, he was dancing to "Wild Thing"—you can't dance to a song like that and not have a little flair in your wardrobe. So when we went in for our fitting, I explained to him that in order to really sell the dance to the audience, we had to look the part.

"I think a little leopard print to convey the whole 'wild thing' theme would be great," I told Tom, who started to laugh.

"If you think that's the way to go, then let's do it," he said gamely. "And you know, I'm okay with a few rhinestones, if you think we need them."

I was shocked. "Really?"

"Well, sure," Tom said. "You're so sparkly all the time, maybe I should have a few rhinestones on my vest for good measure."

I knew he'd catch the *Dancing* bug! It was so great, because like many men who have been on the show, he had an initial inclination to go conservative. But the fun and the fabulousness of the experience is infectious, so before long, they all come around in one way or another. For Tom, it was a pretty quick transformation. He wanted rhinestones, and nobody was going to tell him otherwise—not his wife, not his daughter, and certainly not his old Washington, D.C., colleagues. I was so happy.

During the final week of rehearsals, Tom started to infuse the routine with his personality. He got comfortable with the basic moves of the cha-cha, then added his own flavor to the mix: a few hip moves, a few booty shakes, and a little bit of pointing with his finger did the trick. I assured him that these tiny little moves would go over in a big way with the audience, and he perfected them in no time.

When premiere night rolled around, Tom and I were ready—leopard print, rhinestones, and all. I had a feeling that Tom's mere appearance on the dance floor would stir up the crowd; then the music started and the screaming began. "Wild Thing" is one of those songs you can't resist singing along to, and the crowd started clapping and squealing. As a politician, Tom knew how to work a room, so he played up to the madness like a seasoned pro. At sixty-two, he was the oldest contestant on the show that season, and the risk we faced was that he might look awkward. But there was no awkwardness to his dancing whatsoever.

His moves were sharp and fluid. He rotated his hips in a big circle, and the crowd screamed. The smile on his face said it all: this was fun, and he was having a blast! At the end of the dance, Tom ran and slid on his knees toward the camera—a big finish and a huge hit. By the end of the night, we proved that we wanted and deserved to stick around in the ballroom for a bit longer.

It saddened me when Tom had to pull out of the competition in the third week because of a full-stress fracture in both feet, stemming from an earlier injury. We had a great time together, but not all partnerships can make it to the end. That's true in life as well as on the dance floor.

★ ☆ ★

Long before I hit the ballroom floor, my first steps were in the San Francisco suburb of Foster City, California. I was born Cheryl Stephanie Burke on May 3, 1984, to Sherri Bautista Burke and Stephen Burke. My parents thought it would be cute to give me names that were similar to theirs but unique enough to be my own. There was no rhyme or reason behind it; it just struck them as a way to have a little fun with naming me. *Stephanie* was a play on my dad's name, and *Cheryl*, of course, was a nod to my mom's name. But for a long time, they couldn't decide if I was more of a Stephanie or a Cheryl.

Finally, when I was in first grade, I made the decision for them. "From now on I want to be Cheryl. No more Stephanie," I declared.

My reasoning at the time was very simple. There was already a girl in my class named Stephanie, and I didn't want to have the same name. My parents looked at me with shock and relief, then legally changed my name to Cheryl, and that's who I've been ever since.

I was a headstrong child, and I definitely have my parents to thank for that. My mother was born in the Philippines, one of seven children of a government-employee father and a high school P.E. teacher mother. The island of Luzon, where they lived, is absolutely beautiful but very poor, and my mother's parents struggled to raise their kids and give them a good education. It was a great accomplishment for a family to be able to send its kids to college, and my grandparents managed to put all of their children through the university. It was a huge testament to my family's will and a large reason that my mother has such a strong work ethic.

My mom, fresh out of nursing school, moved to the United States in the late 1970s. Work opportunities were more plentiful and lucrative here than in the Philippines. She signed up with a nurse staffing agency, and anytime a hospital needed someone to fill a shift, she showed up. Most weeks she worked seven days, two shifts a day, and she sent money back to the Philippines to help her parents out as often as she could. She worked first in Tennessee, and then later moved to Los Angeles, which is where she met my father during her early twenties.

My father was a very successful attorney in Los Angeles. He was raised in New York City by his grandmother, which, according to my mom, explained why he was so kind and respectful toward women. He was in his thirties when he met my mother. They both lived in the same apartment building and, again according to my mom, he was instantly smitten with her. She thought that he was charming and had a great sense of humor, but she wasn't impressed enough to slow down for a second look. She came to the United States to work, make money, and build her career. She wasn't interested in dating. But my father wouldn't take no for an answer. He was used to getting his way in objections in a court of law, so how was a woman going to object to going on a date with him?

My father's persistence paid off. The two of them eventually became very good friends, then started dating. During their courtship, my mother's mother became very ill, so my mom traveled back to the Philippines to help take care of her. My dad followed my mom to Luzon and fell even deeper in love with her after seeing how close she was with her family and how she was able to take such amazing care of my grandmother.

My parents had planned to have a big wedding, but when my grandmother died in June 1983, they just had a small civil ceremony at Los Angeles City Hall instead. They postponed their plans for a big celebration with family and friends until the following year, and by then I was on the way—my mother was pregnant with me at the time. I'm told that the party was fabulous, with great food, great music, and lots and lots of dancing.

My mother knew that she was going to have to make some changes in her work schedule, since she was five months pregnant and working double shifts all over the city. Meanwhile, my father had lost a sizable amount of money in an investment that didn't pan out. This bad luck, combined with my mother's need for a career change, sparked the idea for my mom's business, Nurse Providers, Inc.

There was a shortage of nurses in the United States at that time, and my mom knew a lot of nurses from working at all of the different hospitals in town. She found a number of people who were interested in picking up shifts, then she went to one of the hospitals where she had worked and talked to its administrator about setting up a system in which the hospital could call her if it needed a nurse to cover a certain shift. The hospital administrator loved the idea. My mom had a solid reputation with the hospitals because she was an exemplary nurse, so they trusted and respected her plan.

Within two weeks, my mom was coordinating shifts with several major hospitals in San Francisco. She had to cut down her shifts so that she could handle the phone calls—from the house—and the administrative work that came along. She did all this while she was in the final months of her pregnancy with me. In almost no time at all, Mom recouped all of the money that my dad had lost in the bad investment.

Things took off from there, and my mom went from being a nurse to being the CEO of a blossoming company that defied most business models because of how quickly she was making a profit. She was expanding the company as quickly as she could, but the demand was always growing, too. The need was there, and she seized it.

Not long afterward, they moved to northern California, where I would be born and grow up—and where my parents would grow apart.

Although my family's finances were on track because of my mom's growing business, my parents' marriage was rapidly falling apart. My father was traveling back and forth to the Philippines, and he had grown to really like life there. My mother, in contrast, was working on her business and really loved life in the United States. I was less than a year old when they decided to get a divorce.

For the next several years, I visited my father on certain days at his apartment in San Francisco and then went back and stayed with my mom at her condo in Foster City. The back-and-forth really confused me. Eventually, my dad began to see another woman. I was so young, but I recall the details as though it happened just yesterday. During one of my visits to his apartment, he sat me down in his big brown leather chair in front of the television with a stack of graham crackers and a cup of milk. Even though I had a pillow propped behind me, my feet barely dangled off the edge of the chair. My father patted me on the head and said, "You let me know if you need anything, sweetie, okay?" I nodded my head as he walked away.

I became bored with *Sesame Street*, and it occurred to me that I was sitting in the living room all by myself. I started to wander through my father's apartment, looking for him. His bedroom door wasn't closed all the way, so I pushed it open to see if he was there. He was—kissing and hugging a woman who wasn't my mom. I didn't know what to make of it, but I knew it made me sad. My eyes filled with tears as I ran back to the living room and climbed back onto the leather chair. I sat there and stared blankly at the TV until it was time for me to go.

My father never saw me at his bedroom doorway, and I never brought it up. I didn't tell my mother about it, either. It was and still is one of the most vivid memories of my childhood. I was already confused about why my parents were living in separate places. Why was I being driven back and forth to visit with them individually? And now they loved other people, too?

My father eventually sold his law practice and moved to the Philippines, then later to Thailand, where he now owns a number of popular clubs. I think it was a very big step for the two of them to realize that their marriage wasn't working out, but they did their best to keep me out of their disagreement.

I have to give my mom credit for making it a priority for my father and me to stay in touch over the years, despite the distance between us. She wanted to make sure that we kept our family ties as strong as possible, so she organized family trips in order that the three of us could spend time together. I don't talk to my father as often as either of us would like, but when we do connect by phone, it's as though we pick up right where we left off. My mom has sent him magazine articles and DVDs over the years so that he can keep up on what I'm doing, and I know that it makes him very happy. He always tells me that he's proud of me, and it's really wonderful for me to hear that.

Even though my father moved out, my mom found a way to keep our house full of life and love. As her business went from a start-up in our home to a thriving corporation, Mom was so busy that she hired a nanny to take care of me while she worked. Her name was Isabel Garcia, but we called her Ima, a Filipino term for "mom." Ima and I became very close while my mom worked and traveled (Nurse Providers now had offices in San Francisco, Los Angeles, and Seattle). I was lonely at home, and if I hadn't had Ima, I don't know what I would have done.

My mom tells me that after she and my father divorced, I had a delay in speaking. She took me to several doctors, psychologists, and therapists to see what was wrong with me. At one point she took me to a hearing specialist because she thought I might be deaf, since I didn't really respond when she spoke to me. It turns out that there were several factors at work. First, the person I responded to on a regular basis was Ima, who spoke to me only in the Filipino language, Tagalog. To this day I can understand the language even though I can't speak it.

Second, it was determined by one of the psychologists that even though I was only eight months old when my parents split up, I sensed the turmoil and the change in our home. It caused confusion in my developing brain, which was compounded by my parents' speaking only English to me while my nanny spoke Tagalog. I had a classic case of delayed development, which apparently is common among young children of divorced parents. By the time I was three, a therapist was routinely visiting our home and working on getting me to speak and respond to things. She recommended that my parents focus on one language at a time with me.

That didn't happen, but I did eventually and slowly emerge from my shell, and it became clear that I didn't really have developmental issues. Still, despite everyone's dogged efforts, I was painfully shy.

My mother was working twelve-hour days at this point, which was very difficult for me to comprehend. I often saw her right before school, usually at the breakfast table, but when I came home from school, she was still at work, and by the time she came home, I was already fast asleep. It was a difficult time for both of us. My mom wanted so badly to be with me, but she also had the huge responsibility of running her company and getting much-needed nurses into short-staffed hospitals. I didn't understand it then, but I do now. I know that she was doing all that she did so that she could provide for her family. That was her way.

I was very fortunate that Ima was there for me when my mother couldn't be. Ima and I became very close. Anywhere she went, I went. When she made dinner, I sat in the kitchen with her. When she took a shower, I sat on the bathroom floor and waited for her to finish. After school, she met me at the corner bus stop and we walked home together. One of our favorite things to do was to find a rock to call our own, then kick it down the street the whole way home. It was our special little game, and I loved it. I always felt so safe with and so loved by Ima. We watched television together, then she bathed me and put me to bed.

I was glued to Ima, and my mom was becoming very attached to Bob.

I'm very blessed because I have two dads in my life. My other dad is my mom's second husband, Bob Wolf. My mom met Bob when I was about four years old. She was taking a music appreciation course to expand her horizons, and one of her assignments was to go to the opera and the symphony and identify the different instruments. My mom belonged to a group called Perfect Strings, which paired people up to attend formal functions. She and Bob love to make the corny joke that they "struck a chord" with each other on their very first outing, because they've been together ever since.

Eventually, Mom and Bob decided that it was time to introduce their respective families to one another. So I met Bob and Mandy, his daughter from his first marriage.

I was focused on getting to know Bob a little better. I knew that he made my mother very happy, so I figured he must be a nice guy. I also was excited to meet Mandy. She was five years older than I, and it was so exciting to have a big-sister figure in my life.

My first real memory of Bob and Mandy is kind of funny. I remember going from Bob's dental practice, where we all met up, back to his house, where he had a golden retriever named Tawney. My mom isn't a huge fan of dogs (I think it's because the dogs she knew in the Philippines were all biters), and she managed to pass her phobia of dogs on to me. We all hung out at Bob's house a bit, and that's when things went awry.

Mandy and I were getting along great, and then Tawney appeared. I looked at the dog and the dog looked at me, and chaos ensued. He just wanted to sniff me; I was the new person in the house, and he simply wanted to check me out. But I was convinced that he wanted to eat me for dinner, so I started running as fast as I could—through the house, out the door, and into the yard. I tripped and fell, rolling and screaming down the hill while Tawney playfully romped after me. Despite that crazy first day, I grew to like Bob a lot. Eventually the dog and I warmed up to each other, too.

The four of us would play games, such as who could run to the car the fastest. It was a silly little thing, but Mandy and I loved our family competitions. Every year around Christmas we would all go to see *The Nutcracker Suite* in downtown San Francisco. It was freezing in the city on those nights, but even when it was snowy and icy I still wore the fancy black patent leather shoes that went with my cute little dress. One night we were running to the car, playing our silly family game, and I was beating everybody. My cheeks were chilled, but I was so happy because I was winning. What I didn't realize, however, was that everyone else was running slower because the pavement was slick. As I ran full-speed, I lost my footing and fell, sliding as if I were on a waterslide. I zoomed right up to—and partway under—our family's car. It was uncanny how I stopped sliding right at our car. I heard about that one for a long time. But hey, at least I won.

Mom and Bob got married in the backyard of our Atherton home, where we'd moved once Mom and Bob started dating seriously. It was really casual. I remember that Mandy and I were part of the ceremony, which I thought was really exciting. I was thrilled with my new family, but even though Bob was the nicest man in the world and treated my mother and me like gold, I was still a little reluctant to open up to him. Once he scolded me for something minor, like getting up from the table without asking if I could be excused.

"I don't have to listen to you. You're not my dad!" I screamed, in an awful display of childish behavior.

It took me a couple of years to accept Bob as a father figure. He was so nice and didn't force a relationship with me, which is ultimately what drew me to him. I can't remember when exactly I started to call him Dad, but at some point I did, and that's because it came naturally. I felt very comfortable around Bob, and we had some pretty great talks, one of which consisted of my insistence that he and my mom expand the family. My demands grew out of selfishness. I was feeling lonely because Mandy had moved to Arizona to be closer to her mom's side of the family, so I begged them to please have a baby—for me.

It's not as though they didn't want to. My mom and Bob were very much in love and wanted to have a child together. But it was considered risky because my mom was forty. I prayed to have a sibling I could play with, and I was so happy when my mom got pregnant. When she gave birth to my beautiful baby sister, Nicole, I was in awe. Nicole was so cute and sweet. In many ways, I looked at her as though she were my baby. The minute I woke up in the morning, I'd rush to see her in her crib. I wanted to pick her up and hold her. Much as Ima took care of me, I wanted to take care of Nicole. I was nine years old, and this baby gave me purpose. She made me feel needed.

As I was growing up, my mom was very adamant that I try almost every physical activity: tennis, soccer, skiing, horseback riding, and dance. She believed that being involved in these activities would help me to overcome being so shy and introverted. I liked tennis, but I wasn't much into riding or soccer because of the mud. It rains quite often in northern California, and I just didn't like being out in the damp and the muck.

Ballet, however, was indoors, so I didn't have to battle the elements. This was my first foray into the dance world. I began when I was four, and I loved its beauty and elegance. Even when I was a child, I loved the discipline that ballet required. I thought that ballerinas were so delicate-looking yet so strong and refined. I took to ballet rather quickly. The instructor complimented me on having such good coordination for a young girl, and the harder I worked, the better I became.

Once I hit puberty, I decided that ballet and I were not made for each other anymore. But my mom, ever the director of the household, was insistent that we all have something that we liked to do. "It's good to try different things to see what we enjoy in life," she always said.

My mom's thing was dancing. She wanted to be a dancer when she was little, but her family couldn't afford to give her lessons. When she became an adult, once her business took off, she was able to finally pursue her passion, and she found that she really enjoyed ballroom dancing. One of Bob's friends also enjoyed ballroom dancing and talked Mom and Bob into going to a local competition. Mom thought that I would like it as well, because there were a lot of younger kids doing it, so she dragged me along on future trips.

At first I wasn't impressed, but soon I told my mom that I was done with trying to fit in the ballet world. Ballroom was where I truly belonged.

Despite being able to assert myself in choosing my extra-curricular activities, I was still very shy and didn't fit in at all, anywhere I tried: the dance studio or school. I rarely talked in school, and I always sat in the back of the classroom. In grade school, it's common practice for the kids to have their eyes checked with standard vision tests. My exam showed that I was very, very nearsighted. My teacher told me that I had to move my seat to the front of the class, and even worse, the eye doctor said I needed glasses.

I hated wearing glasses. I was always teased by the other kids. They called me "monkey" because my ears were big and I had full lips. It wasn't anything especially mean; it was just kids being kids. But I was very sensitive and that teasing destroyed any self-confidence I had. I already never wanted to talk to any-body; then suddenly having to wear glasses just made me look even more like the dork the other kids thought I was.

I used to "forget" my glasses, and my teacher would lecture me: "Cheryl, you need to remember to bring them to school every day. Otherwise you're going to strain your eyes." That didn't have much of an effect on me. She tried another approach: "Cheryl, how do you expect to get good grades if you can't see your assignments?" I didn't care. I was so sick of being teased that not being able to see or get good grades were the least of my worries.

In the midst of this struggle, I received the devastating news that Ima had become very ill. She was having severe abdominal pain and couldn't stand up, so my mom took her to the hospital, where the doctors ran all sorts of tests. After a couple of days, Ima received the grim diagnosis that she had stage four breast cancer and that it had spread throughout her entire body. "There's not much we can do but try to keep her comfortable," the doctor told my mother. "She doesn't have long to live."

I went to the hospital feeling confused and scared. I was twelve at the time, and all I could do was wish and pray that this whole grown-up situation would just disappear. I wanted to have things go back to normal at home. I couldn't comprehend what was going on and why it was all happening so fast. There was no time to really get a grasp on things.

Ima's wishes were to return to the Philippines to be with her family, and my mom arranged that in no time. Within days, Ima and my entire family were on a flight to the Philippines. How could we not go with her to make sure she got home safely? How could we not give everything to this woman who was not just a nanny but also a beloved member of the family?

Ima died just a few weeks after we got her back home. I had never experienced the death of a loved one before. I didn't know how to process the feelings, so I put on a stoic facade and bottled up my emotions. I didn't want to cry. I didn't want to acknowledge that Ima was gone. It was too painful to go through, because it was like losing a mother or an older sister. I tried to distract myself with TV and dancing and sleep. Sleep became an escape mechanism, and it helped me to cope with Ima's death, the teasing from my classmates, and the frustration I had because I was going through puberty earlier than most of the girls my age.

I was so lacking in self-confidence through elementary school and middle school that I never wanted to draw attention to myself. I was a pretty good student, but I didn't love school. I showed up on time, did my homework, and got good grades. That was all.

I never wanted to flaunt my parents' money or success. I just wanted to be normal. I didn't have a lot of friends, but the kids I did spend time with lived in comfortable, middle-class neighborhoods and weren't obsessed with having the latest, greatest car or going to every concert that came to town. I was already different enough that I didn't want my parents' slightly more affluent lifestyle to make me seem even weirder. When I was at home with my family, I had a completely different life, dancing and competing on weekends (more on this in chapter 3). Almost no one at my school knew that I was into dancing. I used to leave school early on Fridays to travel to competitions, but nobody really bothered to ask why I was leaving early.

That all changed my junior year of high school. My school, Menlo-Atherton High School, was having a big fashion show, and Neiman-Marcus and Macy's were sponsors. My mom volunteered to be on the fashion show committee, and she suggested to the show's choreographer that instead of having people just walk down the runway wearing their cute outfits, they should spice things up a bit with some dancing. She didn't have to do much convincing at all. Everyone loved the idea of doing something different from the norm to make the night fun and memorable.

I had a great dance partner at that time from Finland named Vesa (you'll hear more about him later in the book), and he and I agreed to dance in the fashion show. He was very into fashion and picked out two incredibly glittery ballroom costumes for us to wear during our performance. I was a little nervous, because even though I danced in competitions every weekend, I had never danced in front of anyone at my school before. But deep down I was excited because Vesa and I were really good together. We knew we had a great cha-cha routine that was going to blow everybody's minds.

That night we took to the stage, sparkling from head to toe. We danced down the runway, and the audience went wild. It was a little flirty and a little sexy, and people were on their feet, whistling and clapping. I think that when people heard we were ballroom dancers, they thought they were going to see something old and conservative and corny, but we had great

CHA-CHA-CHA TIP

To execute the cha-cha-cha, you need good hip action and fast footwork. You also need great timing to really feel the music in your body.

music and great outfits. Nobody had ever seen anything like that before at my school. People who had never talked to me at school before that night came up to me and raved. "Oh, my God! I never knew you could do that," one girl gushed.

I have to admit that it felt great. It was like a little debutante ball for me. I finally "came out" as a dancer and showed the school what I liked to do. I didn't hold back—and people liked me for it! I met several girls who quickly became my friends that night, and teachers came up to me to commend me for working so hard to develop my talent. Even the principal made a point to thank Vesa and me for sharing our gift with the school.

Take a risk and reveal your hidden talents.

That night was a big turning point for me, because it gave me the confidence to let everyone into my world. I finally felt comfortable with people knowing who I was and what I was about. My shyness still reared its head from time to time, of course; in fact, it has never completely gone away. But that night, I was proud of my efforts and my accomplishments, and I wasn't afraid to flaunt them. My mom was so proud, too. It was a night none of us will ever forget. I finally took a little risk—just like Tom DeLay would with rhinestones and "Wild Thing" years later on *Dancing with the Stars*—by showing a side of my personality and talents that no one had really seen before. And that risk, even with a simple dance like the cha-cha, paid off—for both of us.

THE JIVE

The Ballroom World

A fun dance full of energy and movement, the jive has a celebratory tone that is often associated with youth and rebellion. It's a variation of the jitterbug, a form of swing dancing that was popularized in the 1950s by girls wearing poodle skirts and boys wearing rolled-up jeans and white T-shirts. It's one of the five international Latin dances and was developed in the early 1900s in the African American community. The quick-paced dance includes a lot of bouncing, leg flicking, and hip rocking.

Ballroom dancing hardly seems to be a symbol of youthful rebellion. But for me, it eventually became just that, because my mom and I were at odds about what role dancing would have in my future.

"You can't dance forever, Cheryl," she liked to remind me. "If you want your father and me to keep supporting you financially, you're going to have to finish college." It was a frustrating conversation, not only because she was the one who had pushed me toward ballroom dancing as a child, but also because my heart just wasn't in the psychology and English classes I was taking at the community college just to make her happy.

I would drag myself to class and try to stay awake, but I didn't care about what I was listening to. I really did try to become passionate about it. I tried to convince myself that maybe I would want to be a psychologist, but in the end, I simply couldn't muster the emotional investment that was required to see it through. My mom really wanted me to get a business degree and take over her company, but I couldn't get excited about that, either.

The only thing I cared about was dance, but my parents insisted that I had to have a profession. So, at nineteen years old, I turned into a professional dancer.

To turn pro as a ballroom dancer, you don't have to pass a formal test to gain certification or rank. Instead, you simply make the decision to change your status and then declare it to the governing body. Up to that point, I had been competing mostly in Pro-Am competitions, in which professional ("Pro") dancers are paired with amateur ("Am") dancers. I was the amateur, which meant that I was the only one being judged. I decided that I wanted to go up the next level and partner with a professional so that we would be judged together as equals. In the ballroom dance world, once you partner with a professional to be judged at that level, you become a professional, too. There's no going back to amateur status.

It wasn't what my parents wanted for me, but I knew I had to take control of my own life and commit completely to the path I'd chosen—no inhibitions, no regrets.

If there's one thing that is a challenge for me every season on *Dancing with the Stars*, it's conveying to my celebrity partners that it's okay for them to do the occasional move that they might think looks silly but that the audience will love. I have to give this pep talk every season.

"The crowd loves to see the unexpected," I explain. "We'll make your routine as precise and as technically accurate as possible, but we need to add some little pieces of pizzazz to each dance to make it stand out from all of the others."

Sometimes the pizzazz is a booty shake. Or maybe it's a funny hip bump, a gesture, or jazz hands—well, maybe I'll leave the jazz hands to Bob Fosse. It's these little things that make an enjoyable dance an unforgettable dance for the audience.

But for some men, ballroom dancing is already so far outside their comfort zone that the extra bit of flair is over the edge. Every season, without fail, the same conversation happens: "Don't make me wear low-cut shirts. Don't make me wear form-fitting Lycra pants. No spray tan. No sequins. And definitely don't do anything that makes me look anything less than masculine." The bottom line from every partner I've had on the show is "Please don't make me look like a fool!"

As any fan of *Dancing with the Stars* can attest, none of our male pro dancers look at all feminine. These guys are the epitome of masculinity, with their sculpted bodies and their pure, raw strength. Even so, there are some male stars on the program who have some reservations about the showier aspects of the performance.

One of those guys was my season four partner, Ian Ziering. Of all the celebrity partners I've had on the show, he is the one I was most familiar with beforehand, because he was one of the stars of the TV show *Beverly Hills, 90210*. My little sister and I loved that show, and I still catch it on reruns every now and then when I need a blast of nostalgia.

When Ian and I met for the first time, we talked about the different types of ballroom dances and how we could really excel at them, especially since he was in such great physical condition. I was really impressed with how carefully he monitored his diet and exercise regime. He liked to run and work out at the gym, and he definitely had the physique to prove it. I encouraged him to do more flexibility exercises, because although he had strength and stamina, he also needed to be as limber as possible to execute some of the moves we'd be doing on the show.

"I'll do whatever it takes," he agreed, "but just don't make me do anything silly. I don't want to look like an idiot."

"Trust me, Ian," I assured him. "You won't look silly."

Nevertheless, Ian had his reservations, and he communicated that with his body. Week after week I tried to help him to let go of his inhibitions and just go with the flow of the dance. In the middle of the season we danced the samba, and I told him to shimmy. It's just a little fun move that riles up the crowd like nobody's business, and I knew that people would especially love it coming from him.

But Ian just wasn't feeling it, despite my pleas. He didn't think that it would carry a great deal of entertainment value— at least, not enough to outweigh how silly he would feel doing it. He nixed the shimmy and insisted that we stick to a straight samba with no extra flair.

What could I say? I never want my partners to do anything they're uncomfortable with, so I relented. Ian consistently got solid scores on his dances, but every week the judges commented that they felt he was holding back. They knew he was good, but they also thought that he could be doing a bit more to make his dances stand out.

One week Bruno Tonioli told Ian that his movements were at times stilted and rigid. He made some joke about how the television show *Grey's Anatomy* has a McDreamy and a McSteamy, and *Dancing with the Stars* has a McStiffy. The nickname was meant to elicit laughter from the audience—and it did—but I could tell that it bothered Ian, even though he didn't let on. I felt so bad for him. I knew he had what it took to really stand out, but I just couldn't convince him to let himself go completely—until we came upon the jive in the semifinals.

As I explained the fundamentals of what a jive entailed, I noticed Ian smiling a bit. "The jive is about a sense of rebellion," I told him. "You've got to just throw your inhibitions out the window. The teenage bad boy doesn't care about what anyone else thinks, right?"

It was as though a switch had flipped inside him and he saw a bright light. "I like this. I want to go for it," he said. "Let's just go for it. No more holding back."

We talked about capturing the fun and frivolity of the dance as well as how we could create a character to get into the dance. Our music was "All Shook Up" by Elvis Presley, and Ian was practically giddy about looking the part. He wanted an Elvis wig, Elvis sunglasses, and an Elvis outfit. He was enthusiastic in a way I'd never seen him before. Ian worked incredibly hard on all of our dances, but this dance was different. This one unlocked something inside him. I think that because he's an actor, he got excited about playing a character while dancing. That was the hook he needed to really connect with the dance.

Don't focus on what others think—rebel!

We rehearsed the jive all week, and I'm sure it was the most fun that Ian had on the show. Every day he came to rehearsal with a renewed sense of energy and enthusiasm. Usually by that point in a season, after nearly three months of working together, my partners and I hit a wall of sorts. It was like a marathon; as we neared the end, we did all we could to muster up the energy to rehearse and learn our new dances.

This dance, however, was like a shot of vitamin B_{12} for Ian. He had found a new source of energy, and he was ready. It still makes me laugh when I think back to how much he was champing at the bit the day of the live performance. He wanted to put on a show for the audience that had supported him all season. He wanted to prove to the judges that he had more to give to the dances and that he was not McStiffy. Most of all, I think he wanted to prove to himself that he could truly master not just the dance but also the performance.

As Ian and I took our places on the floor, Ian beamed with excitement. He assumed Elvis's swagger and cool, then midway through the dance he suddenly started doing the loosest, most fluid hip gyrations I'd ever seen him do. He did really well in rehearsal, but he absolutely nailed it in the live performance! He played to the crowd's wails and whistles. The judges grinned and clapped along. When we finished, our bodies were drenched in sweat, and we were greeted with a rousing standing ovation from the audience that sent chills through our bodies.

By finally giving his all to the performance, Ian had accomplished what the judges had been telling him all season. Not only had he danced an amazing jive, he also gave the dance a new level of entertainment value that left the audience wanting more.

Our jive earned a perfect score from the judges: three tens, our first and only perfect score of the season. Ian and I jumped up and down and hugged each other as the judges held up each card. The crowd wailed even louder. Then the show went to commercial, and the other dancers mobbed us backstage. They congratulated Ian on earning a perfect score, and the male pros commended him on his impeccable showmanship.

Despite our performance, though, we were eliminated on the results show and didn't get to advance to the finals. It was disappointing, after our tremendous breakthrough, but even so, it didn't get me down. I was so proud of Ian and all that he had accomplished. He ignored what was going on in his head and let his body do the talking. That was indeed a victory, in my mind.

☆ ☆ ☆

Every dance I do comes from something inside me that is completely natural. When I dance the jive, it's a happy feeling, but it's also a real feeling. When I dance the *paso doble* ("double step"; see chapter 5), it's a sort of anger that I have within me that I show with my movements. That's why getting into dance was incredibly important for me. It allowed me to truly express myself.

It wasn't always this way, though. When I first got into ballroom dance, I started with a group class and almost let my thoughts and inhibitions hold me back. I was twelve years old, and my mom took me to the Imperial Dance Studio in Redwood City, California. It was about a ten-minute drive from our house in Atherton. My mom thought that the group classes would be a good way for me to dip my toes into the water, so to speak, to see if I liked ballroom dancing.

She picked me up from school one day, and we drove to the dance studio. I felt ambivalent about it. Most of my dance training was in ballet, and this seemed to be the same sort of thing, with slightly different music. I couldn't really get that excited about it. My mom, on the other hand, was extremely excited, because she was in love with the elegance of ballroom dancing—especially the slower, more graceful dances like the waltz.

The group classes went well, but I was still undecided whether ballroom dancing was for me. There were a lot of older people in my class, and I felt out of place. It felt weird to be learning dances with people who were old enough to be my grandparents. I just wasn't quite sure that the ballroom was really going to be a place of self-discovery for a teenage girl.

My mind changed after my mom took me to a dance competition that was just a short drive from our home. We took our seats in the competition hall, and I began to survey the room. It was a Pro-Am competition, and I could not believe the number of dancers who looked my age. I definitely noticed the young, cute guys dancing with young, pretty girls. There was makeup. There were costumes. There was music. Was there ever music!

The music really got me going. In ballet, we tended to dance to a lot of classical music. Rehearsals were often very quiet and intense. I found the ballroom world to be totally different. The crowd clapped along to the music, and the dancers fed off the energy of the crowd. The dancers showed their emotions on their faces. Their sequined costumes caught the light at different times and angles and made their dances come to life even more. Another plus is that there were no tights. I hated wearing pink ballet tights, so I loved that there was not one pair in sight on the ballroom floor. I was hooked! I was mesmerized by it all, and I wanted to be part of it.

"Mom, I really want to do this. I think this is really for me," I said excitedly.

"You think so?" my mom asked.

"I really do. I think I want you to sign me up for private lessons like you talked about a couple weeks ago," I said. "I want to be the person who entertains the crowd. I know I can do this. I really want this."

I know it was funny for my mom to hear me talking like this. For weeks and weeks she had been pushing me to try harder with ballroom dancing, and I had been, well, a typical twelve-year-old. I didn't care to work that hard for something. What kid at that age has the focus or the discipline to study and practice something that intense? Actually, there are quite a few such twelve-year-olds, and after that first competition, I became one of them.

My mom talked to several people at the dance studio about me taking one-to-one lessons. The person whose name kept coming up was an instructor named Rex Lewis, so my mom reached out to him, and he said he'd like to meet me.

I started taking lessons with him right away. He was a great guy and an incredibly patient teacher. But he was in his mid-fifties, which made him an absolute geezer in my eyes and definitely made me question whether what I was doing was totally uncool. Nevertheless, twice a week after school my mom would drive me to the dance studio so I could practice. Rex taught me how to do the cha-cha-cha, the waltz, and the *paso doble*.

As I grew as a dancer, I began to look forward to our rehearsals, because at each practice Rex commented on how much I was improving. He told me that I had great posture and grace as I danced. He said that my movements were fluid and natural, not stilted or premeditated. He started to feel like a grandpa to me—a very spry, incredibly agile grandpa. The positive reinforcement did wonders for my confidence on the dance floor. Soon I didn't care whether I was cool. I just wanted to keep dancing.

After a few months of taking lessons and practicing twice a week, I entered my first Pro-Am competition. Rex entered the two of us in the International Grand Ballroom. Rex would be the "pro" in our set, of course, and I was the "am." We danced all of the Latin ballroom dances, including the *paso doble*, the cha-cha-cha, the samba, the rumba, and the jive. Looking back, I know that Rex was the perfect person to take me through the steps of my first competition. If only I had had the *Dancing with the Stars* makeup and the wardrobe team behind me then!

I still cringe when I think about what I looked like that day. I was never much of a girly-girl, and what I know now about hair and makeup I certainly didn't know back then. All I really knew how to do was to pull my hair back into a ponytail, so as a result my ears stuck out a bit. I had no idea how to put on makeup, either, so I didn't put much on. I had a brown velvet costume with big cutouts on the sides by my waist, but since I hadn't yet discovered the beauty of spray tanning, I just ended up looking pasty.

Despite not looking as polished as I would have liked, and despite not winning, I did discover that I absolutely loved the thrill of being in a competition. It was so much fun that I couldn't wait to do it again—except with a younger partner. As much as I adored Rex, I knew, when I saw all of the other younger dancers and their partners at the Pro-Am event, that it was time for me to change to someone who looked like a more natural match. It just seemed to be a better fit for everyone involved.

Soon after, I changed instructors, from Rex to several younger professional dancers at Imperial. I also changed my focus to really concentrate on the Latin and rhythm dances, which were a bit quicker-paced and more exciting to me. I started doing showcase dances with Tony Delgado, a professional rhythm champion. My mom kept telling me how fortunate I was to be partnered with such a prestigious pro dancer, but I was twelve and didn't have the perspective on things that she did.

I also started working with another pro by the name of Stephan Krauel, who taught me the Latin ballroom dances. He co-owned Imperial Dance Studio with Rex and was what's called a Ten Dance champion, which means that he was a champion in both the Latin and the ballroom dances. It's rare that dancers can master both kinds of dances, because they have such different styles, and the work to perfect just one style is hard enough. Mastering both is nearly impossible.

Then there was Jonathan Roberts, who is now one of the pros on *Dancing with the Stars*. Jonathan and I trained in ballroom dancing together, and we even competed in a few Pro-Am competitions as a pair. He was only a few years older than I (I was thirteen at the time) and already a seasoned pro. Jonathan was so kind and helpful, much as he is on the show with his celebrity partners. He was patient, understanding, and extremely supportive. He really helped me to grow as a dancer.

Jonathan could tell that I was committed to becoming the best ballroom dancer I could be, so he suggested that I observe people whose dance abilities were superior to mine to help me improve. While Jonathan and I were at one competition, he introduced me to David Bruckner.

David was about four or five years older than I, as I was just hitting high school age, and he was paired with his teacher, Christine Belanger. Together they were everything I wanted to be. Christine was gorgeous, and she danced so beautifully that it made me want to cry. She was in her early twenties and sexy, sophisticated, and sleek. And she was dancing with my dream partner.

I was fascinated when I watched David dance. He was a rising star in the Pro-Am world, but just as important, he was cute. All I could think about was how wonderful it would be to get to dance with David. He was like a ballroom god in my eyes.

I told Tony and Jonathan that I would die for a chance to dance with David, so they talked to Christine and arranged a tryout for David and me. In ballroom dancing, the chemistry between dancers is crucial. At that time, *chemistry* was just a science class I struggled with. I had no idea that in the world of performing arts it meant that two people were so in tune that they conveyed passion and unity in every element of their performance.

Finding a partner means investing in someone with both your time and your money. Ballroom partners must commit to each other by always adhering to a strict rehearsal schedule, no matter what. Because I was so young and inexperienced, it was a big deal that David and Christine were willing to even entertain taking a chance on bringing me into the picture, and I was so nervous that I might blow my big chance.

One afternoon, David and I met at a studio while Tony and Christine gave us a routine to work on together for a couple of hours. We talked through the routine and rehearsed while Christine and Tony observed our interactions. I was the new girl in town, so my fate was completely up to Christine and David. Christine was the "It Girl" in the Bay Area dancing world, so she was the one who was basically going to tell David, "Yes, Cheryl is good enough for you" or "No, Cheryl isn't ready to dance at your level."

I thought that the session had gone well, but I analyzed and overanalyzed it the whole way home. I wondered if they would want me. I wondered if I was good enough. I could not stop thinking about how great it would be to become partners with David.

Several days passed after the tryout before I got the call. I was talking with my parents in their bedroom when the phone rang, so I rolled over on the bed and picked it up. It was David. I nearly screamed.

"Cheryl," he said. "I was so impressed with you at the try-out the other day. I'd really love to dance with you, if you're interested."

I didn't know what it meant to be cool and relaxed. I was too over-the-moon with excitement.

"Of course I want to dance with you!" I shouted. I was so giddy that I started running around like a little kid who had just gotten the best news of her life. It really *was* the best news of my life, at that point: I had found something I wanted more than anything, I had put my mind to it, and I had gotten it. I was starting to learn that if I wanted something to happen, I should just go for it with everything in me. It seemed like a dream.

Then my mom brought me back down to earth. "Cheryl, you have David for a partner now, but this is serious," she warned. "You have to practice all the time. You can't slack off."

Mom was right. I was going to have to practice all the time. No skipping practice or just halfway trying when I got to the studio. This was a big step for me to take, and I didn't want to screw it up. What's more, I was a big risk for David to take, and I didn't want to let him down. For the first time in my life, I learned what discipline is all about. I wanted to skip the practice and head straight to the

You need to work at what you love.

performance. It's not that I hated to practice; I just preferred to dance in front of people more. I loved performing. But dancing with David would teach me what it means to really work at what you love.

For the next four years, David and I grew together as dance partners and friends. He lived in Marin County and I lived in Atherton, which was about an hour and a half away by car. David would often come and pick me up after school in his little red Honda Civic and drive me to practice. When we had a late night or a weekend competition, my mom would let him stay overnight in our guest room.

David and I also hung out all the time with his best friends, Genya Mazo and Giselle Peacock. I was having the best time of my life. The four of us were practically inseparable, which was rather unheard of in the cutthroat world of competitive ballroom dancing. We really had something special in our friendship.

Genya and Giselle lived in San Francisco, and the four of us Bay Area kids would compete all around the world. Genya and Giselle were so much better than David and I; they always beat us in competitions, but we didn't think twice about it, because we were so excited for them and for our own development as dancers.

As I became more passionate about my dancing, my mother's credit card got more of a workout. Ballroom dancing is a costly sport, and it's not at all lucrative. People who compete do it not for the money but for the love of dancing. My parents completely understood that I was crazy about dancing, and they encouraged me to continue with it; however, my mom did have some legitimate concerns about how much she was spending on my training, my competition entry fees, and my travel expenses—not to mention my shoes and my costumes.

It was a situation that all four of us—Genya, Giselle, David, and I—faced with our families, who supported us as much as they could. We had decided that we wanted to travel to London to train and compete over the summer, but the reality was that if we wanted to go to England we'd have to raise our own money.

My mom and I struck a deal. She told me that she would continue to support me in what I wanted to do, which was ballroom dancing, if I continued to do well in school. But if I wanted to go to England, I would have to earn my own money to pay for my flight and my living expenses there. She said that she'd continue to pay for my dance lessons and shoes and costumes, but I would have to take on some of the financial responsibilities.

At that time, an hour of coaching with a top pro in England cost about 80 pounds, which was equivalent to about $150. And because such a long trip was required, it made sense to stay in England for an extended period, so the food and lodging costs would add up quickly, too. That's why a lot of dancers from the San Francisco area made England an annual summer destination. London was kind of like summer camp for ballroom dancers.

But it wasn't just London that was expensive, it was the entire sport. Ballroom dancing costumes are often $1,500 each;

dance shoes run about $140 a pair; then there is makeup, false eyelashes, spray tans, hairspray, and more. The average entry fee for a dance competition is about $30, and every couple usually does a minimum of five dances per competition. If you win a competition, you might get a $1,000 check to split with your dance partner.

It doesn't take a mathematician to figure out that the numbers are pretty tough. Most dancers are not wealthy. They work very hard, and every penny earned goes right back into their dancing: training, costumes, and entry fees. Ballroom dancers keep up with the sport because they have the passion and the drive to do it. I had that drive, and I was determined to do my part to ensure that I could continue with the one thing that meant the world to me.

Committing to pay for my summer in England was a valuable lesson for me. It taught me that if I really wanted something, I could have it—as long as I worked hard for it. My mom was not one to hand things out on a silver platter. I had to take ownership of my wants and my needs. "That way," she explained, "you'll appreciate it even more."

She was right. David, Genya, Giselle, and I devised a plan on how we could raise money for our trip doing what we did best: dancing. We all piled into David's car and headed down to Union Square in downtown San Francisco. It's a culturally diverse part of town where a lot of artists—singers, dancers, mimes—perform in the hope of getting donations from passersby. We made signs that read "Please support us. We're raising money to train with the best in England." We had a boom box blaring music, and we literally danced in the streets at Union Square. People honked their horns, clapped, and (much to our surprise) donated quite generously.

The four of us also put on a dance camp. David had the idea that we could fly in some of the top coaches in the country to teach dance students at what was then Starlite Dance Studio in Mountain View, California. (It's funny, because now, ten years later, I own that studio—it's called Cheryl Burke Starlite.) The students paid fees to cover the instructors' travel expenses and teaching costs, and we received a percentage of that money to put toward our fundraising. It was an amazing success! Between dance camp and our street dancing efforts, we ended up raising a few thousand dollars, which was enough to cover our airline tickets to England and a tiny flat.

We had enough money to rent two rooms in a small house in the outskirts of London. The girls had one room and the guys had the other, plus we had an adult chaperone with us at all times. We all shared the food we brought with us because we didn't want to spend what little cash we had left on anything but dancing lessons. Now that I'm much more aware of nutrition, I cringe when I think how unhealthy it was to eat instant maca-roni and cheese every day for weeks. But we were just so happy to be there that food was the last thing on our minds.

That summer was such a bonding experience for the four of us. We continued our friendship and cheering for one another in competitions for several years after that. Yet as is often the case in the ballroom world, after a few years David and I "broke up." That's what it feels like when you stop dancing with someone—a sad, depressing breakup. You have spent so much time together rehearsing, performing, traveling, and eating; your families have gotten to know each other really well; and you've had a really special relationship with the person who is the other part of your dancing unit.

Then as soon as you go your separate ways, you don't really talk to each other anymore. It's sad when a partnership ends, but in the case of David and me, we both just decided that it was best for us to move on to other partners in the dance world so that we could grow in different directions. I haven't talked to David in a while, but I treasure the time we had together and the special friendship we had.

I didn't have a steady dance partner for a while after that. In fact, I went through several partners while I was in high school. I just wasn't clicking with anybody.

I learned later that my partnership with David was rare in the ballroom world. People generally don't compete together for years and years. It's common to change partners as often as once or twice a year. That's just how it goes. And after David, that was how it went for me, too.

✰ ✰ ✰

I've mentioned it before, but I really can't emphasize too much just how wonderfully supportive my parents were, especially my mom. She drove me to all of my lessons, rehearsals, and competitions, and she was always coming up with creative ways to help me develop my talent even more.

One year, while I was in high school, my parents were doing some remodeling of the house, and they suggested giving the living room a hardwood floor so that we would have a place to practice. It wasn't just me dancing by this point—my little sister, Nicole, had picked it up, and even my parents enjoyed a turn or two around the ballroom. Never one to go halfway on anything, though, my mom soon changed her mind. Rather than just having a small space with a wooden floor, why not redo the entire area to create a full ballroom?

Once she made the suggestion, we were all on board. It would save my parents hours of driving Nicole and me to and from practice, and it would also give us the opportunity to rehearse whenever we wanted to. It was perfect—if only I had someone to partner with.

Finding a new dancing partner in the Bay Area who was a good match for me was a huge endeavor. Most American teenage boys are just not into ballroom dancing. In Europe, though, it's a different story. It had become an annual tradition for my mom and me to travel to London for the Blackpool competition every year, and we met so many dancers there from around the world who dreamed of coming to the United States.

One of the friends I made was a French dancer named David. We were great together on the dance floor, so my mom offered to let him live in our guesthouse if he wanted to come to the United States to work and compete. He jumped at the chance, got all of his documents in place, and found a job at Starbucks as soon as he arrived in San Francisco. During the

day I was at school and David worked, then in the late afternoon and the evening we rehearsed together.

This went on for about six months, and I was excited to see
how well we were working as a unit. When Christmas came
around, David went back to France to visit his family, and he
decided to stay there. He told me that he was really sorry, but
he missed his country terribly, and being back home made him
realize that he didn't want to live overseas after all. I was crushed.

After David, I had another international partner who lived
with my family. His name was Vesa, he was from Finland, and
he was fabulous. We hit it off like old girlfriends right from the
start. He was so much fun to talk to, and rehearsing had never
been such a blast. He was a phenomenal dancer and very easy
to get along with. Even better was Vesa's boyfriend, Luca. He
was from Italy and just as much fun to be around as Vesa. They
knew so much more about fashion, hair, and makeup than I
imagined was possible—and I really needed their help.

Even after several years in the ballroom world, I knew next
to nothing about those fashion and makeup, so I happily followed Vesa's and Luca's advice as they made me over and taught
me how to really embrace the glamour of ballroom style. Vesa
designed and sewed many of our costumes for competitions;
Luca accessorized them with rhinestones and other embellish-
ments. Vesa had a natural flair for fashion, and he helped me
to understand how the outfits could actually enhance our performances.

Vesa also did fun things with my hair. He gave me updos,
curls, swoops, and bangs. He even taught me how to properly

apply makeup for maximum effect. I learned how to camouflage my freckles with foundation so that I would look a little older on the dance floor. My freckles were fun and cute in everyday life, he explained, but competitive dance judges don't go for "cute."

Vesa also showed me how to embrace false eyelashes, which was a huge accomplishment, since I used to dissolve into tears when I had to try to put them on. I just couldn't do it—I was so afraid of poking myself in the eye. But Vesa helped me to learn how to have fun with it all, so that dressing up and looking the part finally became an enjoyable aspect of getting ready for competitions.

Vesa and I stayed together for about a year and a half. We had an amazing time, but we both eventually decided that it was time move on and pursue our respective passions. I continued with dance while Vesa shifted his energies entirely to fashion. I was so sad when we had to say good-bye, but everything worked out for the best. I'm making my living as a professional dancer, and Vesa is an extremely successful dressmaker in London, designing gowns for many of the world-champion ballroom dancers. My partnership with Vesa was definitely one of the most fun experiences I've ever had in the dance world, as well as educational. He put me in touch with my glamour-girl side and taught me how to achieve the sleek, glamorous look I'd been missing. I'll always have a soft spot in my heart for him.

I was still a teenager, just seventeen, so instead of trying to find yet another partner after Vesa left, I decided to focus on high school for a while. I didn't have a lot of friends, but I did have a boyfriend at the time, and I managed to go to my homecoming and my prom. It was nice to have some of those normal high school experiences despite my crazy schedule. But because all of my time was spent at the studio, in competitions, or with my boyfriend, I didn't really start to have real friendships with the other girls at school until we were nearing graduation. I just didn't have the free time to hang out at the mall or go to football games on Friday nights. It was a little disappointing, but I knew that I would have to sacrifice something if I was ever going to reach my full potential as a dancer.

As soon as I turned eighteen, I connected with the person who would help me do just that: Allan Tornsberg.

Allan and I had met when I trained in England. He was a ballroom champion and was regarded as one of the top ballroom coaches in the world. Even Maksim Chmerkovskiy, one of my fellow *Dancing with the Stars* pros, took lessons with Allan at one point. I just happened to be celebrating my birthday while he was visiting San Francisco, so I went out on a limb and invited him to the party. He was one of my all-time ballroom idols, so when he showed up, it was the greatest birthday present ever.

We talked for a while about my dancing goals, and everything just clicked. He took me under his wing and completely reshaped me as a dancer. It was like learning the ballroom all over again. Allan made me throw out all of the techniques and bad habits I had acquired over the years, and I learned how to do things flawlessly and technically perfectly. I had never worked so hard at dancing, but to this day I credit my success to Allan's careful instruction.

Allan and I traveled the world, literally. He invited me to come along as he coached others in Denmark, Russia, and England so that I could absorb every partnering and every style possible. When Allan wasn't giving me instruction directly, I observed him teaching others. I was at the studio with him sometimes up to ten hours a day as he taught other aspiring dancers. It was the best learning experience I ever had, and it set the stage for the next big step in my career.

I did a year of community college to make my parents happy, but it just wasn't right for me. I finally decided that I wanted to partner with a Latin dancer in New York City named Jose Decamps. Allan trained me, and his partner, Vibeke Toft, trained Jose. Allan and Vibeke arranged for a tryout for the two of us, and the chemistry was there—in more ways than just on the dance floor. Both of us believed that we'd met the perfect partner as we competed all around the country, so we also started dating.

It wasn't long before I packed up my things and moved across the country to New York. Jose and I lived in a little box of an apartment in Harlem. We had the bed and the couch sandwiched next to each other, with a TV, a computer, and an efficiency kitchen crammed in the rest of the space. We had two small niches that were considered the closets, and since my things didn't fit, I just stacked them on the floor. This was the furthest thing from plush, but I was pretty happy because I was on my own, supporting myself by teaching dance.

JIVE TIP

You have to be light on your feet and have lots of energy to keep up with the kicking and flicking action your legs will be doing in the jive. And you better have stamina, because you won't get a chance to stop and catch your breath!

I developed a steady clientele, and with each competition I acquired more students. My mom was impressed with my entrepreneurial venture, but she was still concerned that the dancing profession was just a temporary one for me and that I needed to find a more reliable line of work.

Jose and I made barely enough money to cover the nine hundred dollars for the monthly rent on our tiny apartment, but for me it was enough. I didn't just have a job; I was pursuing my passion for dance and making a career out of it.

4

THE SALSA

Parties and Paparazzi,
Reputation and
Responsibility

Because salsa is arguably one of the most popular dances on the club scene, couples of all ages love to go to salsa clubs to dance. The spirited, get-on-your-feet music is often performed by a live band. Think nightlife, crowds, and not a care in the world. The salsa is believed to have originated in Cuba, but different versions of the salsa incorporate influences from Puerto Rico and other Western Latino cultures. In ballroom competitions, the female partner usually wears a revealing two-piece, midriff-baring outfit, and the male partner often wears a low-cut shirt and very form-fitting pants. Salsa is fast-paced and very fun, requiring both partners to incorporate leg and arm movements, spins, and shimmies. More advanced salsa dancing involves acrobatic moves and lifts.

Salsa dancing is considered a staple of nightlife activity. There are salsa clubs jammed with people every weekend in cities all around the world. Nevertheless, that scene was still pretty new to me as a twenty-one-year-old. I knew how to dance a variety of dances when I was a competitor—but to actually dance in a club? I wasn't sure that was really my thing. I just didn't do it much at all. I was still a pretty shy person off the dance floor. I preferred to keep to myself, with a very small circle of friends.

When I moved from New York to Los Angeles in late December 2005 to start working on *Dancing with the Stars*, I didn't know a soul. My boyfriend and I had been on the outs, so when I took a job three thousand miles away from him, that pretty much ended the relationship. I was excited about my new job but nervous, too. I had never been on television before and I didn't like cameras. I was second-guessing whether this was the right career move for me. I was a competitive ballroom pro, and with enough work, I might become a professional champion. Did I make the right move?

There I was, sitting in the one-bedroom apartment the show had provided me, in January 2006, and feeling a little lonely, a little homesick, and a lot like a fish out of water. One of the producers on the show knew that I was adjusting to Los Angeles rather slowly. After a group meeting with the season two celebrities and dancers, she gave me her number and said that if I ever wanted to go out to dinner, to a movie, or for drinks to give her a call. I was so shy about trying to reach out to anyone, but one Sunday afternoon I decided to break out of my shell. It was very unlike me to initiate a social outing, and I'm sure I sounded really nervous when I called her and asked if she wanted to do something that evening. I was so proud of myself after I hung up, though, for being proactive in trying to make friends.

We decided to hit what was a hot spot at the time, a club called Hyde. A few of the other pro dancers from the cast went to the club, too, and we all hung out and talked and shared a bottle of wine. At one point I thought, "I should probably get going," but then I realized that I didn't have to go home. I didn't have a curfew! I didn't have a jealous boyfriend who was going to be wondering where I was or what I was doing. I didn't have to check in with anyone to make sure it was okay that I was still out with my new friends. I felt as though someone had given me a get-out-of-jail-free card. We stayed out for hours and had a blast.

I couldn't help but remember that first night in Los Angeles whenever we did the salsa portion of the show. Most of my partners on *Dancing with the Stars* have told me that they have danced in a club at one time or another. Loud music and happy people moving together to music is exactly what salsa is all about. So when it was time to teach the dance to my season eight partner, actor Gilles Marini, he got very excited. "I love to dance in clubs!" Gilles cheered.

The salsa was one of our last dances together on the show. Gilles and I had a wonderful streak of high scores and audience support, which was truly gratifying to him because he was one of the lesser-known celebrities who competed on the show that season. He was featured in the *Sex and the City* movie as the guy who bared all in a scene with actress Kim Cattrall. But to *Dancing* fans, Gilles was known for giving his all on the dance floor.

As we approached the semifinals, some reporters commented on how Gilles's abilities on the dance floor were almost on par with those of some of the male professionals. He and I were flattered—and a little nervous—to hear that. It's a good position to be in, but it's also a precarious one. We felt the pressure to improve our performances even more, but as we reached the end of the season, Gilles was dealing with a lot of pain. Ever since the second week of rehearsals, he had been nursing an injury to his left shoulder; by the time we got to the salsa, his shoulder was so inflamed and tender that he could barely lift his arm. He knew that he was going to have to have surgery after the season was over, but his goal was to go as far as we could on the show.

The great thing about Gilles was that he didn't want to give up. The bad thing about Gilles was that he didn't want to give up. It was a catch-22, because if I pushed him too hard, I knew that his injury could worsen and he'd be unable to compete at all. But because we had already set the bar high for ourselves by getting top-notch scores all season—including a perfect score for our tango in week four—we had to push ourselves. If we didn't continue to perform challenging choreography, the judges would call us on it. And even more important than the judges' opinions were the opinions of the fans. The last thing Gilles wanted was to disappoint our fans by giving them a performance that was anything short of spectacular.

As luck would have it, one of our dances for the semifinal round was the salsa. It's a great dance for someone of any age and any ability because it has only three steps. That's it: one, two, three—and then you repeat it over and over to the beat of the music. The male partner leads the female partner, but she does all the spinning around on the dance floor, and he just basically continues the rhythm with his feet. The couple changes directions on the dance floor, but it's the man who leads the woman into the fancy moves. In salsa clubs, it's common to see older men dancing with younger women. An experienced man can simply lead the woman around the dance floor, twisting and spinning her as they go. As long as he can keep the beat, he doesn't have to perform any tricks to make both partners look good.

Gilles and I checked out a club in Los Angeles to study the feel and pulse of the dance. As the choreographer, I had to make sure that Gilles didn't need to use his left arm and shoulder too much, but I wanted him to see all the other things he could do to give our dance flair. The song that was given to us was Pitbull's "I Know You Want Me (Calle Ocho)," a catchy hip-hop tune that can be adapted very well to doing the salsa. Gilles instantly felt the music and began to add his own flavor to the dance. He wanted to add more hip action, more shimmying, and more moves in which he would slide on his knees. He didn't want to pamper his left shoulder as much as I thought he should. He insisted on going all out.

"Cheryl, I am going to have surgery on my shoulder regardless of how we dance." He shrugged, in pain even then. "I know you are concerned, but I will be fine. We need to go all out for the fans. They are the ones who kept us here. I get e-mails all the time from people saying how much they enjoy watching us dance, so I want the semifinals to be our way of saying thanks to the fans for supporting us all season long."

I loved his dedication, and I think that's a big reason we had such incredible chemistry when we danced. Off the dance floor Gilles was a lovely man, completely enthralled with his family and a wonderful friend to me at the show. But when we were performing, people always commented on how intensely connected we appeared. Gossip blogs even speculated whether we were dating. At first it made me angry, but Gilles and his wife, Carole, loved that people were thinking that way, because it meant we were doing a good job with our storytelling on the dance floor.

Gilles and Carole were both sure that our salsa would blow everyone's mind, because the chemistry between the partners is what really sells the salsa to an audience. We felt good about our salsa as we went out onto the dance floor, because we knew we had that chemistry, we knew we had the dance down, and we knew we'd have fun.

Gilles and I gyrated our hips and shimmied like nobody's business to get the crowd going. When we turned our backs and shook our booties, the place went wild. We were in step every moment of the dance, and we knew it, the crowd knew it, and the judges knew it.

One of the judges, Carrie Ann Inaba, stood on her feet and cheered for us, which was a huge compliment. She and Bruno Tonioli both exclaimed that we "deserved to be in the finals." Len Goodman told us that he was at a loss for words. "I'll just say this—I wish I had an eleven paddle," he said. (The paddles, with score numbers on them, go up to ten.) Gilles and I were humbled by the high praise. We were humbled even further when the judges all lifted up their paddles to reveal three tens. It was our second perfect score of the night (our first dance that evening was the waltz), and Gilles and I were speechless. We celebrated by having a wonderful dinner with our families and friends. It was a night that neither of us will ever forget.

As I readjusted to life on the West Coast after moving back from New York City in order to do the show, I got into a routine. It was my first season on the show, and during the day I rehearsed with Drew Lachey, my season two partner, then went to my apartment to shower and have dinner before meeting up with the gang around nine or ten at night. We stayed out for a few hours, hit a club or two, and then sometimes headed back to someone's place to grab a bite to eat and a chat before turning in for the night.

For the most part, things were pretty fun and low-key. The cast and the crew were really tight. We all enjoyed spending time together, and even after the season ended, we often got together with one another for dinner and drinks.

At about the same time, I hired a publicist named Susan Madore. I was virtually anonymous before *Dancing with the Stars*, but after I won with Drew that season, I began getting recognized a bit. Press requests were coming in for me, and I decided that I wanted to hire Susan to help manage my publicity. She became a great adviser; her first order of business was to make sure that I stayed in the public eye in between seasons two and three. The second season ended in late February 2006, and the third season wouldn't hit the airwaves until September. Susan wanted to make sure that I was out and about during that seven-month stretch.

"You don't want people to forget who you are, Cheryl," Susan insisted. "You won the show, and you want that momentum to carry over to next season. Plus, you could use a bit more experience doing interviews at red carpet events."

Susan's plan was to make sure that I attended movie premieres and charity events. She thought it would help people to remember my name and also to remind them that *Dancing with the Stars* would be back on the air in no time. I felt safer in a group, so I always took a friend along wherever I went. We wore cute summer dresses, walked the red carpet, and talked to the reporters and the camera crews. Some of them were the same people I had talked to when I was on the show, so the familiarity helped ease my nerves a bit.

Before long, I became a little more comfortable doing interviews. I was asked what I was doing over the summer, how I liked Los Angeles, where I put my trophy, and whether I thought I would win the show again. It was all pretty easy and fun. Los Angeles started to feel a little more like home.

When season three began, people told me I hit the jackpot by being paired with Dallas Cowboys running back Emmitt Smith. Everyone in town was buzzing about how great it was that the football legend was going to do our show. What a coup for us! But I had my doubts. I have to confess that I didn't even know who Emmitt Smith was, what he looked like, or that he was known for his fancy footwork on the football field. Instead, I had the image of a clumsy giant who would not be able to twirl, hop, or glide to save his life.

I was dead wrong about Emmitt. We did our first live show and danced the cha-cha-cha, and I knew he was going to go far. He was so attentive and disciplined during our rehearsals, and he also had undeniable charisma. He was a natural in front of the audience, with his huge smile showing how truly happy he was to be dancing on national television. It was fun to watch and infectious.

Sure enough, Emmitt became a legend on the dance floor. Season three was a huge success, with a big finale showdown between Mario Lopez and Karina Smirnoff and Emmitt and me. On a chilly November evening, Emmitt and I were declared the season three champs, narrowly beating out Mario and Karina. Just as earlier that year, when I won season two, the band played, the crowd cheered, and confetti fell from the ceiling. But this time I felt prepared to handle everything that comes along with winning. Press interviews? No problem. Autograph requests? Sure, I'd be delighted to sign photos. It wasn't so scary this time. In fact, it was a lot of fun.

The night we won, Emmitt and I were whisked away on a private plane to New York City to do the live morning show circuit. As we made the rounds, I realized that I had the same makeup on that had been applied almost twenty-four hours earlier. On finale day for the show, there are so many people who need to have their hair and makeup done that things start very early in the morning in order for everyone to be ready to go live on the air to the East Coast. I had gotten my makeup done at eight in the morning, before the final; after the show, I went directly from the studio to the airport and boarded the plane to New York. It was a red-eye flight, so we dozed until we landed, then we were whisked by a car service to ABC to go live on *Good Morning America*.

On top of my day-old makeup, I had an enormous pimple growing on my forehead, and it was all I could think about. At each place we visited, the makeup staff would dab a little concealer and a little powder on my forehead in an attempt to camouflage the zit, but nothing could contain it. After *Live with Regis and Kelly*, Emmitt and I were taken to our hotel, where we checked into our respective rooms and crashed. I was so exhausted.

The next morning we were due to make an appearance with Rachael Ray, and I still had the same makeup on that had been applied forty-eight hours earlier. I know it sounds gross—and it is—but the alternative would have been to have someone who had never met me do my makeup, just a few seconds before we went on camera. Besides, if I had done my makeup in the morning, that would have cut into my sleep time, and I was in a terrible state of sleep deficiency.

We did Rachael Ray's show, and I was so excited about being there, but I was also incredibly self-conscious about the Mount Everest–sized blemish growing on my forehead. Every time we had a commercial break, the makeup artist would come over and dab a little more foundation on the zit. Rachael kept telling me not to worry about it, but I knew better. I watched that show later, and you could spot the zit as plain as day. How embarrassing (but funny) it is now. At the time, of course, I was mortified.

That week in New York was surreal. Emmitt and I were celebrated everywhere we went. People waved as we walked down the street. Drivers honked their horns and hollered at us from their cabs. I felt on top of the world.

When I got back to Los Angeles, I did what I had started to do more frequently, which was to socialize with my friends. We hit the club scene, dancing and laughing to our hearts' content, then we went home. The only thing different now was the small assemblage of photographers outside the clubs. My group had its favorite haunts, and these became known to the paparazzi. Just a few months before, we'd been pretty much ignored.

Now that *Dancing with the Stars* had reached a new level of popularity, the paparazzi were taking notice not only of what the celebrities were doing but also what the professional dancers were up to. The photographers, most of them men, knew all of our names. They'd shout out to us when we arrived at the club. We'd wave and talk to them and sign autographs. We naively thought, "Hey, this is pretty cool that these guys want to take our pictures and put them in magazines. And they are so nice!" And they were, then. I didn't understand yet the games that they play.

☆ ☆ ☆

That winter, *Dancing with the Stars* went on tour around the United States and Canada. The show had become so popular that a natural next step was to assemble a cast of past celebrity contestants and professional dancers to perform in cities all around North America.

The prospect of us taking the show on the road was exhilarating, because dancers have long been relegated to the background in the entertainment industry. Think about it: singers like Madonna and Jennifer Lopez have "backup dancers." Backup. Background. Behind. That's how most dancers' careers go—we are just a piece of moving scenery. But on this tour, we were in the spotlight as much as the celebrities were, and it was magical. We performed to sold-out arena audiences every night.

After nearly every show, we rode the adrenaline rush of the crowd as we boarded the buses and traveled to the next city on the tour, and we were so pumped up that no one could sleep. Instead, we had wine and cheese parties, played loud music, and did what we did best—dance. We had so much fun on the road that the party continued when we returned to Los Angeles to start working on the show's fourth season.

The cast of season four included some very fun people, including my close friend and fellow pro dancer Kym Johnson and her celebrity partner, Joey Fatone. Maksim Chmerkovskiy was part of the mix, along with my dear friend and colleague Tony Dovolani. We often went out to dinner or to clubs after a Monday night performance show, since at the time, Monday nights at *Dancing with the Stars* were for us like Friday nights for the rest of the country: it was the end of the workweek. We rehearsed with our partners all week in preparation to perform live on the Monday night telecast, and once we were done we could take a breather, knowing that we could finally sleep in on Tuesday morning.

Depending on which friends or relatives were in town, the circle would widen, and our group would hit the town en masse. It was a blast. All of my life up to that point had been about being disciplined, working hard, and staying focused. This was the first time in my life that I felt a nice balance between working hard during the day and having fun at night. Of course, the paparazzi were watching our every move.

Susan began getting phone calls at her office from magazines and Web sites asking about my comings and goings. The same thing happened to a few of the other dancers. One day when I was driving to grab lunch, I had the distinct feeling of being followed. There was a pickup truck that turned whenever I turned, and it scared me to death. I was near my apartment complex, and I wanted so badly to drive back into the underground parking garage and go into my apartment, but I didn't feel safe. There was no way I was going to let myself get trapped in the garage with a strange man stalking me. I kept driving around for another half hour until I either lost him or he just gave up and went away.

Over the next several months, I became much more aware of the fact that I was no longer anonymous Cheryl from northern California. I was now the two-time *Dancing with the Stars* champ, and every time our gang went out, whether it was for sushi at Koi or drinks at Villa, the paparazzi were out in droves. When we walked up to the doorway of a restaurant or a club, the guys who had once been so sweet to us were now throwing themselves in front of us with cameras and microphones, shouting inappropriate things to try to get a reaction.

Video crews hollered things like "Hey, Cheryl—go easy on the vodka tonight!" or "Is it true you're hooking up with your partner? We hear everyone is sleeping with everyone on *Dancing with the Stars*." Joey Fatone just laughed them off. I think he was used to people shouting at him obnoxiously because it had happened so many times when he was with 'N Sync. But the madness infuriated me. I felt provoked into behaving badly.

One night I was out on a date with my boyfriend, and from the moment we got out of our car until the moment we stepped into the club, the paparazzi were taunting us.

"Dude, did you know your girlfriend likes to party?" one guy asked as he walked backward just a few steps in front of us, his video camera glued to our faces. I rolled my eyes, but the guy continued, "Yeah, Cheryl. You know what I mean. You like to party, don't you? You're out every night."

We finally made it inside the club, and for a couple of hours I forgot that the same annoying photographers and videographers would be outside when we left. As we walked out of the club, the taunts resumed: "Cheryl, what did you drink tonight? Did you save any vodka for anyone else?"

I made a rather vulgar suggestion to the cameraman about what might be a better use of his time, but this only riled him up more.

"Just ignore them," my boyfriend muttered under his breath as he paid the valet parking attendant.

A long wait began, because the car had to be brought to us from around the block. I had spoken back to one paparazzo, which gave him an in with me, and now I—we—simply couldn't get rid of him. He and the others formed a semicircle around us. They filmed and photographed us second after agonizing second as we waited for our car. By the time it finally arrived, after about three minutes, I was infuriated. As I climbed into the car, I let loose, cursing like a sailor at the paparazzo, who still had his camera trained on me. I'm not proud, but there it was. The fame game was officially no longer fun.

The rest of season four was just the same: fun on the set but headaches with the paparazzi. Eventually I learned to ignore them as they taunted me, but when I stopped acknowledging them, that's when the taunts and the insults really increased, in the form of exaggerated photographs and Internet reports.

For example, I went out with some friends for dinner, and when I came out of the restaurant, my heel caught a crack in the pavement, which caused me to stumble slightly. I lost my footing for only a nanosecond, but the next day there were photos of the incident along with reports that I had left the club falling down drunk. I couldn't believe that they could turn something that small and meaningless into a headline trashing me.

Susan called me to ask what had really happened. She knew that I was not a stumbling drunk. I told her the truth, and she gave me fair warning. "Watch where you go in the future, okay? You need to go out, and you need to let your hair down, but you can't be careless when you walk out, because there are cameras watching your every move."

I understood what she meant, but I truly had done nothing wrong, and the unfairness of it all was so frustrating. I was busting my butt working fourteen-hour days, and I just wanted to go out every now and then to have some sense of normality in my life. I felt penalized for acting like a normal twenty-three-year-old.

The hounding continued, but it wasn't until the summer of 2008 that things really turned ugly. I had just wrapped up season six with Cristian de la Fuente, making it to the finals even though he had suffered an arm injury. I was facing the first summer I could remember that held no work obligations, no tours, no competitions, and no boyfriend. I was free to do whatever I wanted to do, and a family vacation in Hawaii seemed like just the thing.

It was a wonderful week of sleeping in, lounging on the beach, bodysurfing, and getting spa treatments with my little sister. When we got back to Los Angeles, I was feeling relaxed and rejuvenated in a way I hadn't felt in years. I looked forward to having a nice, quiet summer ahead of me in Los Angeles without any professional responsibilities looming over my head.

My quiet summer didn't last long. I went to a beach party in Malibu right around the Fourth of July, and I took a friend along to spend the day having fun in the sun. It was a beautiful day, and I decided that I'd have a margarita and take a little stroll along the water to enjoy the view. The paparazzi were lurking, of course, and snapped some shots of me as I was walking, but I just ignored them, determined not to let anyone or anything ruin my mood.

The next day a photo ran on several Internet sites. The sites called me a lush, a drunk. My phone rang early in the morning, and it was Susan. Once again I felt defensive for having a good time. I had had one margarita—I wasn't falling down drunk in the surf. A couple of days later, the photo had circulated to even more sites. Several tabloids had picked up on it and were saying that I was partying out of control. There was no way I could have functioned during the day if I was doing all the partying they said I was. It was absurd.

Susan understood this and I understood this, but my parents didn't. My mother, who was five hundred miles up the coast in San Francisco, saw the photos and read the gossip sites. She called me and immediately started to lecture me about how people perceived me. "You're getting a reputation as a party girl, and that's not good."

I had no choice but to defend myself. "I'm a grown woman. I'm allowed to go to a club and hang out with my friends," I told her. "You've been there when you've come to visit. You know that we're not getting fall-down drunk!"

"I know, Cheryl," she reasoned. "But you are starting up your own dance studios, and you don't want people to think that you are reckless or that you make bad moral decisions. You are a health and fitness professional."

I found it extremely irritating that having a margarita on the beach ignited gossip on the Internet and turmoil within my family, but I also realized that my mom was right. Even though a lot of the celebrity gossip on the Internet is severely embellished, many people read it and take it as fact. My first dance studio had just opened in San Francisco, and young girls were looking up to me as a role model. I didn't want them—or their mothers—to think that I was behaving irresponsibly.

I had worked too hard for too long to have a successful career, and I didn't want anything to hurt the reputation of the show, stand in the way of my dream to expand my studios nationally, or keep me from being an ambassador of dance to a whole new generation. There was no way I was going to let a couple of stupid paparazzi photos ruin that. So that was the end of my adventurous nightlife days. I spent the rest of the summer quietly enjoying my time off out of the limelight.

When season seven began, I partnered with Olympic track star Maurice Greene. We focused on the show and on dancing well. In my free time, I concentrated on creating my own line of dance and fitness clothing and expanding my dance studios. If the paparazzi were waiting for me outside the Los Angeles hot spots, they were disappointed.

I still go out every now and then, but I don't stay out very late. Instead, I usually just invite a few friends over to my house to sit in front of the fireplace and talk. The club scene is too loud and chaotic, anyway. I have discovered I'd rather sit in a quiet place and have a normal conversation instead of having to shout over loud club music. The lack of cameras chronicling my every little move is nice, too.

I had my taste of the paparazzi, and now I know how to handle them. They used to ask me questions and I'd answer them, naively thinking it was the polite thing to do. But now when they try to goad me into an exchange, I simply choose not to answer them. They call me names and try to taunt me, like whiny kids on the playground. "You're such a b———h. Why are you being such a b———h?" one videographer recently snapped at me when I ignored him while I was out to dinner with my boyfriend. "You used to be so nice," he said. When the videographer made those comments, I just kept on walking quietly. The paparazzi were left with a bunch of boring

> I have learned that with the press, as with a lot of things in life, less is more.

SALSA TIP

There's a lot of hip action and body pulsing in the salsa, so quick feet are a must. Women also need good flexibility and the ability to spin fast without getting dizzy.

footage of my boyfriend and me getting into my car and driving away. They were annoyed, and I looked good—that's what I call a good night out on the town!

It takes incredible discipline on my part to ignore the paparazzi's comments, no matter how rude or inane they might be. There are some very kind and considerate photographers and videographers out there, but when I'm in situations with annoying paparazzi, by choosing to say less, I'm able to have more control. Even though I may be seething on the inside, I will not let my body language or my facial expressions communicate it.

THE *PASO DOBLE*

Fighting Back

The Spanish dance *paso doble*, which means "double step," is full of passion, confrontation, and domination. It is often referred to as the bullfighter dance because the male partner usually takes on the role of a matador and the female partner emulates the bullfighter's cape or the bull. The male partner takes the lead. He is superior and dominates the female partner, who follows him. Resist as she might, the female partner is subdued by her dominant male counterpart. When executed properly, the tension between the two partners is palpable.

The *paso doble* is the dance in which I tell my partners to channel all of their pent-up aggression. When I performed with Gilles Marini in season eight, he was excited about taking on the role of a Spanish matador. Because he's an actor, he really connected with the storytelling of each dance.

But this dance was different, I explained to him. "In this dance, I really want you to feel the tension between us," I said. "You are going to dominate me and I'm going to resist, and the more I resist, the more determined you will get."

"I can do it," he said. "I have a martial arts background, and some of these movements are very familiar to me."

When Gilles and I rehearsed, we liked to go all out. He wanted to know exactly what was expected of him and precisely how much he needed to exert himself to master the routine for the live show.

Our routine had sections in which we did flamenco and stomped our feet on the floor; other sections included sensual moves. There were also aggressive moments in the routine, which conveyed anger, competition, and confrontation. There was a definite push-pull theme throughout the choreography before the end, when Gilles, in the role of the matador, "killed" me, as the bull. It was very intense and very memorable.

Throughout the week as we rehearsed, I started to develop bruises on my wrists and my hips. In one part of the dance he would roll me on the floor with his foot; it was very physical, and my hips hit the floor hard every time.

"Cheryl, I do not want to grab you and throw you so hard," Gilles pleaded with me. "This doesn't feel right."

"It's okay, seriously," I assured him. "Just do it. You're not hurting me."

The truth is that I *was* hurting. I was sore. But we were developing our performance, and the last thing I wanted was for Gilles to hold back. He was so much taller than I, which made the domineering aspect of the dance all the more palpable. The music was very intense and helped to define the tone of the dance.

On show night, the adrenaline pulsed through our bodies, and the intensity with which we rehearsed was really amped up. We performed our roles, and the crowd loved it. The judges loved it, too. We received a nearly perfect twenty-nine out of thirty points for our performance. Most of all, Gilles, who was always hard on himself, was happy. I felt the after-effects of the dance for the next two days, but what's a little soreness for the sake of entertainment? We knocked it out of the ballroom.

☆ ☆ ☆

The *paso doble* is a dance I've long enjoyed performing. I love its layers and its sense of fervor. I've often been asked how it is that I can take on the role of the dance so convincingly. I think it's because in my own life I have been in the position of having another person dominate me.

I've had more than my share of unhealthy relationships. The person I am now is not the person I was when I was in my late teens. I was always shy and insecure growing up, and it wasn't until I started dancing that I emerged from my shell. But that was on the dance floor. In social situations, I was never a leader and was almost always a follower. I'm ashamed to say it, but I didn't like to speak up, and as a result I allowed myself to be pushed around and manipulated by the guys I dated when I was younger.

I had two boyfriends when I was in high school, and both of those relationships were abusive. The first guy I dated had gotten his ex-girlfriend pregnant and then broken up with her. Not long after that, he and I started dating. To say that it was a complicated situation is an understatement, but I craved attention. I didn't want to be alone. So I refused to open my eyes to a bad situation.

He was two years older than I, and I thought that this made him more mature. All it really meant was that he thought he could automatically call all of the shots about when and where we'd go out, when we could talk on the phone, and when we couldn't. When he forced himself on me to have sex, I unwillingly obliged, because I feared I'd lose him altogether if I didn't sleep with him. I hated myself afterward, but he had me convinced that he knew what was best for me.

The relationship continued despite his controlling nature. One day I noticed he had hickeys on his neck. When I questioned him about them, he told me a bizarre and unbelievable story about visiting his ex-girlfriend to check on the baby; they got into an argument, he claimed, and she threw a rock that hit his neck and left a mark. What's even more unbelievable is that I bought the excuse.

He sweet-talked me out of being upset every time I challenged him, and every time I fell for it. "Baby, you're so amazing," he'd say, hugging me and planting kisses on my forehead. "You know you're the one I want to be with." And in no time, whatever it was that had made me angry or upset disappeared.

That kind of toying with my emotions, that kind of mental abuse and manipulation, coupled with my lack of self-confidence, went on far longer than I ever should have allowed it to. Eventually that bad relationship ended, but soon enough I found myself getting into another unhealthy relationship—and this one lasted three years.

In high school, I thought that I knew what I needed and wanted from a boyfriend. I rebelled against my parents' financial success by dating guys from the "wrong side of the tracks." I was attracted by our differences, culturally and financially. I liked the seemingly rough-and-tumble existence of that type of guy: athletic, domineering, good-looking. It was this kind of "stick with me, baby" personality that I was drawn to.

But soon the relationship became less exciting and even scary. My second boyfriend was incredibly jealous and possessive. If I even dared to talk to a male classmate at school, he freaked out. If I said hello to any of his friends in passing, he thought I was flirting with them. He didn't just ask me whom I was talking to and why; he grabbed my arm, slammed me into a wall, and demanded an explanation. No matter what I said, he was furious, and the result was my being roughed up.

It started with insane temper tantrums in which he yelled and swore a blue streak. At first he slammed his fist on a table or pounded on a wall in anger. But the longer we were together, the more his behavior crossed the line into physical abuse, like a punch in the arm or a slap across the face.

I knew in my head that things were not right. I knew that I shouldn't be with a guy like that. But for some reason I thought I could fix him. "I can turn him around and help him," I reasoned to myself. "Then we'll be happy, and everything will be okay." Boy, was I wrong.

One day when I went to his house to meet him for a date, he wasn't home. His parents let me wait for him inside, and when he finally showed up, hours later, I was really annoyed.

"Where were you? Why did you make me wait so long?" I asked.

"None of your damn business!" he snapped back at me.

"What do you mean it's none of my business?" I challenged.

Oh, God, I had gone too far. He was enraged. His face contorted, and he began screaming at me in front of his parents. His mother watched us but said nothing. The more my boyfriend yelled, the angrier he became. I was scared. I started to head for the door, but he grabbed me by the arm.

"You b———h! Where do you think you're going?" he yelled as he unbuckled his belt and slid it out of the loops of his jeans.

I broke away and ran as fast as I could—out the door and across the front yard to the gate. As I tried to open it to run to my car, my boyfriend swung the belt and it hit my arm. It left a welt. I cried and begged him to stop, but he wouldn't. With his mother standing at the front door, still doing nothing but passively watching, he took another swing at me with his belt. This time it smacked across my back. It stung like nothing I'd ever felt before.

I begged him to stop. I screamed and cried for help, but nobody did a thing. The neighbors saw what he was doing, but none of them moved from their porches to help me. His father watched silently, as if he approved that his son was putting me in my place. Finally I broke free, ran to my car, and sped off as fast as I could. He jumped into his car and tailgated me all the way back to my house.

I'd like to say that that's the end of that story, but it's not. We broke up, but in the days that followed he apologized profusely and swore it would never happen again. He tried to convince me that he was the only person who would ever love me, and I was so out of touch, so desperate to feel valued by a boy, that I believed it. We got back together and broke up a couple more times before I moved to New York City.

I've dated nice guys in my life, too. For some reason, the nice guys—the ones who call when they say they are going to call, take me on nice dates, and send me flowers—baffle me. I'm always a little confused when there isn't any drama or huge challenge in the relationship. For a long time, the guys who treated me well left me too mixed up for me to have a relationship with them. I didn't feel deserving of being treated well, and I didn't understand that these guys might give me things or be nice to me without expecting anything in return.

Over the years, I've talked to a lot of psychiatrists and therapists. They all agreed that a big reason for my trouble in mastering the art of healthy dating relationships is a trauma I suffered as a young girl.

I have never spoken publicly about what happened until now, but it's not because I'm ashamed of it or because it still holds any power over me. It has simply taken me nearly two decades to process what happened, why it happened to me, and how it affected my life afterward. But now I am no longer under the control of those memories.

When I was in kindergarten, my mother and my stepdad hired a retired mailman to do some work around our house. He often stayed overnight in a small room in the basement near the laundry room. He was very friendly and outgoing and was very well liked by everyone he met. My parents heard that he was highly recommended, so they trusted him to help out with the family.

He started by doing odd jobs, like going to the grocery store and taking my stepsister and me to and from school. He had an old, beat-up tan van that he drove us around in, such as to tennis lessons or music class.

The more familiar he became with me, the more he asked to spend time with me. Whenever we came home, I went to my room to play, but one day he asked me whether I'd like to watch television with him. "Why don't you sit next to me, Cheryl?" he asked.

I obliged, and he snuggled up next to me, cradling me in his arms. He wanted to be close to me, and I found the cuddling comforting. I know that this might sound odd, but I was only six and still upset about my parents' divorce. I liked the feeling of being held; it seemed to be his way of showing me fatherly love.

This began to happen more frequently, and it quickly progressed from gentle hugs. He started to touch me in his van when he picked me up from school. He pointed out all of my birthmarks and freckles, putting his hands on each one. When we got home, he wanted me to sit with him in his room so that he could continue to be close to me. "Cheryl, come over here. I don't want to be by myself on this big couch," he said.

I sidled up next to him, and he began to stroke my back under my clothes and then touch other parts of my body. Eventually, he started to watch pornographic movies and wanted me to watch with him. I didn't understand what was going on or what I was looking at, but I didn't want him to be lonely. I felt guilty if I didn't stay—as if I would be doing something wrong if I left him all alone.

I'm not sure how long all of this went on, but I do remember the last time I saw him. I was still in kindergarten. He had taken me and my stepsister and her friend somewhere in his van, and he tried to touch them the same way he'd been touching me. They were older and knew that what he was doing was wrong, and they immediately told someone.

Our parents swung into action, furious at what they'd just learned about this man they'd heard so many good things about. I was asked if he had ever done anything to me, and I said yes but that it wasn't wrong. I was so innocent and naive. I thought that he wanted to be close to me because he loved me. I didn't understand that he was doing a terrible thing.

Charges were brought against him, and all three of us girls had to go to court to testify. It was an upsetting time for my parents, because they could not be in the courtroom with my stepsister and me when we testified. They were beside themselves with guilt. My mother sobbed. My dad was a wreck. They felt responsible for this man's actions.

I was escorted into the courtroom while my parents waited outside. I was wearing an oversized black sweater with the number thirteen on the front in neon green. The sleeves were long, and my mother had to roll them up so that when I took the oath my hand would be visible. I kept fussing with the sleeves while I was being questioned because I didn't want to look up.

I was asked to explain what had happened, where it had happened, and how often it had happened. I wasn't sure about any of it. I was so confused by the situation. Everyone kept saying that he had touched me inappropriately, but I didn't understand what he had done wrong, that he had crossed a line with me. I felt so guilty, as though I were a bad person doing something terrible by talking about him to the people in the courtroom. I looked over and saw his face, and all of a sudden, random things—like his favorite color being purple or the fact that he wore jeans with suspenders—flooded my mind. I started to cry, and we took a break.

Then a young woman (his niece) came forward. She lived out of state, but when his family discovered that he was being accused of child molestation, they agreed to testify so that he wouldn't be able to do this to anyone else ever again. This other girl's testimony that he was, in fact, a predator established that

This was the night that changed my life: my first *Dancing with the Stars* championship trophy!

Here I am at one of my first ballet recitals, before the ballroom bug bit me.

July 25, 1993, was a big day of celebration in our house. My mom married Dr. Robert "Bob" Wolf at our home. My stepsister, Mandy, and I got to be bridesmaids at the wedding. Our baby sister, Nicole, just six months old, was christened that day.

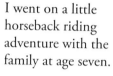

I went on a little
horseback riding
adventure with the
family at age seven.

I'm so grateful for the
family vacations we
took when I was a kid.
Here I am, eight years
old, taking a break
from a quad bike
adventure with my
mom on the sand
dunes in La Paz,
Mexico. We took in
an extremely beautiful
sunset that afternoon.

Here I am at age ten, striking a pose for the camera.

I am eleven years old and in the fifth grade in this class photo.

When I was twelve, I danced a Pro-Am competition with my first American Style Latin dancing instructor, Tony Delgado.

This is me with my first amateur partner, David Bruckner.

I was thirteen when I competed in my first Latin
Ballroom competition with David.

We rang in my mom's fiftieth birthday Brazilian-style in New York City. At the time, I was training in Denmark with my coach, Allan Tornsberg. Allan and I flew in and surprised my mom with a special samba performance. My sister Nicole is in the front; standing in the back from left to right is Mandy, Bob, my mom, and me.

Emmitt Smith and I pose with our mirror ball trophies from season 3— what an amazing night!

Gilles Marini has become such an amazing and supportive friend. Here we are cutting the ribbon at my studio opening.

Lance Bass and I get ready to celebrate New Year's Eve in Las Vegas.

Here I am goofing around with dancer Genya Mazo during the *Dancing with the Stars* tour.

Kym Johnson and I tough it out on the road with the *Dancing with the Stars* tour.

A wonderful night of tango in Buenos Aires was a special treat for my mom and me.

This is me practicing with Gilles Marini and the other finalist couples for the finale of *Dancing with the Stars*.

Mark Ballas entertained us on the charter flight to New York from Los Angeles after the *Dancing with the Stars* finale.

Good Morning America sent a double-decker bus to pick us up from the airport and bring us to the studio. None of us had slept, but we still couldn't have been happier.

Here I am in the green room at *Good Morning America*. The fatigue still hadn't hit us.

Gilles Marini and I perform our dance live on *Good Morning America*.

My friend Jack
Ketsoyan and
I get ready for
a night out.

Maurice Greene and I
wait in the media area
after performing our
salsa. Maurice always
makes me smile.

This is from the Jazzercise photo shoot. Judi Sheppard Missett, the founder of Jazzercise, is an inspiration to so many women.

I am behind the scenes of the making of a Jazzercise commercial. Those workouts are intense!

Taking a glimpse behind the scenes at my shoot in Malibu for Fullfast, you can spot me doing a yoga pose for the camera.

This is my tallest partner, Rick Fox, and me after taping the *Ellen* show.

Me and my best friend and makeup artist, Jojo McCarthy.

Here I rehearse the Argentine tango with the cast of *Forever Tango* in Buenos Aires.

Drew Lachey and I perform our "Save a Horse" dance. It was recently voted the number one fan favorite *Dancing with the Stars* routine!

he had a pattern of abuse. The prosecutors were able to get a conviction, and he went to jail for nearly twenty years.

Since then, I've seen many child psychiatrists and other therapists. There was a big effort to make sure that I talked about what happened and how it affected me. But despite all of that counseling, I never realized then what I realize now. The molestation affected all of the relationships I've had over the years. It had a lot to do with my shyness and insecurity; consequently, I turned to my boyfriends for validation. I had sex at a young age because that's what they wanted and that was my way of showing them love and of feeling loved. As for the pattern of abusive relationships, on some underlying level I thought that's what I deserved.

I moved on from that experience very slowly. I had a pattern of dating abusive men until I was about twenty-one years old and moved to Los Angeles. It was about this time that I started to make a little more money and support myself; that did a lot to boost my self-confidence. It was as though I had experienced a cleansing of sorts, and a healing.

I've kept up with therapy throughout the years, which has done wonders to convince me deep down that I deserve a healthy relationship. Now, if I see any early signs of domination or jealousy—anything that remotely seems to be crossing a line—I'm gone. If I'm dating a guy and he asks roughly, "Where were you last night when I called?" that's a red flag for me.

The odd thing is that I know I can still be needy with men. I seem to be a happier person when I'm in a relationship than when I'm on my own. I want to be an independent woman, but there are times I crave being with someone. I'm on top of the career stuff; it's the personal stuff that's still a challenge. I'm still learning my self-worth in many ways. But I don't necessarily see this as a bad thing. I know I'm constantly working on myself.

In January 2010 my mother came to Los Angeles to visit me. I had just gotten out of a relationship—a very healthy, positive, and loving relationship— with a nice guy. I was sad that things had come to an end, but we had taken the relationship as far as it could go. My mom and I were talking about life and dating, and for the first time, I opened up to her about the abusive relationships I'd been in as a teenager.

We're all works in progress, and that's a good thing.

"Cheryl, my God, why didn't you tell me?" she cried.

"Because I thought I could handle it," I told her.

She was shaken and confessed that she had long suspected that these guys were abusive toward me, but she hadn't wanted to interfere.

We talked for a long time about how I thought that I didn't deserve to be treated well. I told her that it's hard for me to take a compliment from a man because I don't feel worthy of it. She was shocked. My mother and my stepfather have always had quite a harmonious relationship. But for some reason, I had it ingrained in my head that I didn't deserve the same in my relationships.

My mom and I also talked about the molestation. She confessed that to this day she is racked with guilt about what happened. She and my dad feel responsible for having put my stepsister and me in danger with that man. But how were they to know? How does anyone know? He gave them every reason to believe that he was trustworthy, so why would they think he was a monster? I had to tell her that it was not her fault and that I was okay. I *am* okay.

As I've gotten older, I've thought a lot about that time in my life. I've been able to look back with a clearer understanding of what happened and how it affected many years of my life. I understand that many people have a very difficult time overcoming an experience like this. It's not easy. It takes time to heal. Although I am one of countless victims of that kind of crime, I made a concerted choice several years ago that I would not let it stop me from living my life—the life that I deserve. No longer would I allow this experience to control me.

About two years ago, my molester was released from jail. He had had almost two decades to think about what he'd done to me, my stepsister and her friend, and his niece—and maybe even others we'll never know about.

He showed up unannounced at my dad's dental practice one day. "I never did anything to your daughters," he said.

My father immediately snapped into protective mode. "You need to leave right now, or I'm going to call the police."

The man, now elderly and very frail, turned around and quietly walked out of the office. We haven't seen him since.

PASO DOBLE TIP

This is an aggressive dance that requires every ounce of effort you can muster. Your dancing has to have energy and passion, but most of all you have to be able to tell a story through your movements and your attitude.

I have learned that the molestation was not my fault. I did nothing wrong. As a child, it was normal for me to trust a grown-up. That's what kids are taught. But I had to deal with a very grown-up situation while I was still a very young child, and frankly, that sucked. What's more, it was probably as hard on my parents as it was on me. I hate that they anguished over this for so many years.

Letting go of the resentment has been a gradual process, but it's very empowering. Every time I talk about it, it makes me stronger and more aware of what has made me who I am.

I broke the pattern of dating abusive men, which I consider a triumph and a big step toward taking control of my future. I won't ever go back to the dating habits I had before I moved to Los Angeles. My closest friends have all told me how much I've grown and how they admire the woman I've become. I am proud of who I am today. I am strong, and I will not let anyone ever overpower me or control me again.

THE RUMBA

6

Learning to Love My Body

The rumba is the dance of love. It is full of rhythmic passion and sensual movement, demonstrated by both partners. What sets the rumba apart from other ballroom dances is that it's not about fancy footwork. Instead, the rumba emphasizes body movement. It is believed that the rumba was largely developed in Cuba, combining influences from the customs of African slaves and those of their Spanish colonizers. The male partner often wears loose-fitting attire, whereas the female partner's costume is more often sexy and revealing. Throughout the dance, the partners come together as one, then separate, before they slowly and sensually find their way back together. There is a fine line that must not be crossed, for the dance style can be misinterpreted as inappropriate or explicit. It's important for the partners to maintain a slow, sensual pace.

People often say that they can't dance, but that's not really true. As human beings, our bodies are able, by design, to form all sorts of shapes and move in all sorts of directions. The belief that someone can't dance is just a mental block. "You need to give yourself permission to dance, to explore, to let go," I tell my *Dancing with the Stars* partners every season. They often look at me as though I'm crazy. I can sense that deep inside they are thinking, "What do you mean, give myself permission to dance? I'm here, aren't I?"

> Showing up is, of course, more than half of the battle, but having an open mind is part of it, too.

The classic dancer body is lean and sinewy, which is perfect for performing the rumba—and neither I nor my season three partner, Emmitt Smith, have such a body. Emmitt's compact muscular build was perfect for plowing through defensive lines as he ran for touchdowns for the Dallas Cowboys. He is powerful but short. I, too, am rather vertically challenged.

All season, Emmitt defied the odds by coming out and performing one memorable dance routine after another. The fans and the judges didn't expect him to move so gracefully, given his physical shape, but time and again he proved them wrong. By the eighth week of the season, Emmitt was flexible. There weren't any dance moves, fast or slow, that he couldn't learn. We were perfectly poised to tackle the rumba. It requires flexibility, strength, and patience—as well as slow and sensual hip movement. I knew that Emmitt would absolutely bring the house down with his performance.

The obstacle I often face with my celebrity partners in this dance is getting close. Even though they know we are "just dancing," the closeness required of the rumba (remember, it is the "dance of love") can be, at times, a little uncomfortable for people.

I can totally understand where they are coming from. For a nondancer to all of a sudden be pressed up against, and writhing bodies with, another human being that he or she has known only a short time—well, it's awkward.

I'm asked all the time, "How do you not fall in love with your dance partner?" For professional dancers, physical closeness is just part of what we do. It's a normal part of executing a believable performance. When there's dance-floor chemistry between two people, it's great to watch, and that's what we dancers want to create for the viewers. Emmitt and I had a solid friendship and a commitment to do the best we could do on the dance floor. We also had an undeniable chemistry when we danced. Maybe that's because Emmitt, who had become a master at moving his body for his work as an athlete all those years, had given himself permission to dance.

At rehearsal it didn't take long for Emmitt to get into the rhythm of the rumba. It was as though he had been doing it for years. I watched him in the mirror as we practiced; he had such precise control of his body. He moved slowly, carefully, and gracefully, much as a martial artist performing tai chi would move. He looked as though he'd been doing the rumba forever; it just seemed natural for him. Then, as he'd done in many of our other dances throughout the season, he put his own signature on the routine.

It's often hard for people to incorporate their personalities into a dance routine. It's the little unchoreographed extras that give a performance a little bit of flavor, like a secret ingredient that only a certain cook uses, that makes it great. Unfortunately, many people concentrate too much on the steps and forget to enjoy what they are doing. I've had partners who take what I say so literally that they forget who they are—that it's the two of us out there performing as a unit, not just me telling them what to do.

Emmitt didn't have that problem. He was not at all afraid to show his personality on the dance floor. He studied, focused, and concentrated intensely while we rehearsed. But week after week I saw him have his "Aha!" moment, when he'd start to smile and do an extra shimmy or hand movement. These were not things he was taught as part of the routine. Once he had the technique of the dance down, he unlocked the showman inside and became a performer, not just a football player who was dancing.

On show night, we performed our rumba to the Atlanta Rhythm Section's rendition of the song "Spooky." We decided that it would be very elegant if we wore all-white costumes: Emmitt in white slacks, a white shirt, and white dance shoes, and me in a sparkly open-backed, long white gown.

The performance started off really well. Within the first fifteen seconds, Emmitt's sultry saunter from the top of the stage, down the steps, and onto the dance floor had the audience oohing with delight. I caught a glimpse of Emmitt's wife, Pat, sitting in the front row. She was beaming as she watched her husband move as though he'd been dancing all his life.

At the point in the song when the lyrics and the music pause on the word *stop*, I was supposed to slink down Emmitt's right leg and dramatically, to the beat of the music, place my hand on his thigh. Instead, at the word *stop*, I accidentally placed my hand a little bit higher, very close to Emmitt's crotch. I could have died. We were only about thirty seconds into our routine, so of course we kept going. There are no do-overs on live television. But after the dance, I was so embarrassed, and I hoped that nobody had noticed it.

The judges praised the routine. Len said it was classy, which made Emmitt and me very happy. We received a twenty-nine out of thirty points, which was amazing. Once the show went to commercial, I apologized to Emmitt and told him that I certainly hadn't meant to put my hand there. He just laughed it off, reassuring me, "It's okay. I haven't even given it a second thought, so don't worry."

That was wishful thinking. Not more than ten minutes after the show ended that night, a reporter asked me about the risqué "Spooky" choreography. A few people buzzed about my unusual hand placement, and even Pat was asked what she thought about a young single dancer putting her hands on her husband like that. Being such a sport, Pat kindly played it up for the cameras, teasing that she thought her eyes had deceived her. We all laughed it off, but deep down I was a little rattled. I can say with 100 percent honesty that it was not planned!

It's not the first time I've been in an uncomfortable situation on the dance floor. Dancers are taught to move their bodies, to own their bodies, and most of all, to control their bodies. But that can sometimes prove to be a real challenge.

Ballet was my entrée to the dance world, and I loved the discipline it required. I took pride in perfecting my technique at class each week. All of the girls in my class felt that way.

When I was about ten years old, though, things started changing for me. I noticed that my legs were getting bigger. Not only were they more muscular, they were also changing shape. My hips grew wider, and I suddenly developed breasts. I started having my period. I didn't look at all like the other girls in my ballet class anymore. They had stick-thin arms and legs. No waists. No chests. They still looked like tiny ballerinas, while I was getting womanly curves. I just didn't understand why my body wasn't like their bodies.

The contrast between me and the other girls in my dance class became the most real to me when I was eleven and tried out for *The Nutcracker Suite* ballet in San Francisco. A few of the other girls from my ballet class went to the auditions, too. I was so excited at the thought of getting to perform in the same production my family attended every year, but as I looked around the audition room, I saw that I looked markedly different from all of the other girls there.

We were all hoping and dreaming that we'd make the cut— and a few did, but I wasn't one of them. I thought my audition went really well. In fact, the director said I did a great job. But the casting directors told me that I didn't have the "look" of the girls they wanted. The ones who were cast all had thin bodies, long hair, and light complexions—everything I didn't have.

I had such a hard time accepting that reasoning, because I knew that I had performed just as well as the other girls had in the tryouts. It wasn't my dancing that was being judged; it was how I looked. It was the first time I truly felt discriminated against. My mother tried to console me, but I felt humiliated. I didn't want to go back to ballet class. I didn't want to see some of the girls who were chosen over me. I'd had it with the pink tights!

Soon after, I switched to ballroom dancing. People of all ages, all shapes and sizes, and all ethnicities and races do ballroom dancing. I felt welcomed into this new world—the attitude seemed to be "the more, the merrier!" But that didn't mean my body image issues ceased. Like millions of teenage girls in the United States, I obsessed about my body. Whether it's right or wrong is irrelevant. It's just a normal part of modern American culture that most women—and now even young girls—tend to obsess about their weight and other aspects of their bodies and their looks. My curves became more accentuated as I got older. By the time I was eighteen, I had a very womanly figure with some serious curves.

I started being aware of what I ate. I noticed what other girls my age had for lunch: salads. No, thank you. I would take a bowl of pasta over a salad any day, and a couple of slices of warm bread with butter. By the time I turned twenty, I noticed that what I ate tended to "stick" to me, and I resented it. Why was it that my metabolism wasn't like other girls' metabolisms? They splurged on hearty dinners—steak, potatoes, and dessert—but I worried about my grilled-chicken salad with light vinaigrette dressing on the side. The more I danced, the more calories I burned, but my curves didn't go away.

On some days I lived with it just fine. On other days I wished that my legs were longer and leaner and that my hips were just a bit narrower. Like many women, I tried everything I could to keep my weight down. I exercised every day. I also monitored what I ate very closely, trying all kinds of diets. I cut out the carbs I love and all fried foods. I ate only fruit before noon. I even had a diet-meal delivery service at one point. But no matter what I ate, I was still self-conscious about my body.

When I started on *Dancing with the Stars* in 2006, my body image issues intensified. I was even more aware of how I looked, especially dancing on television. I hated watching myself on TV. I thought that the costumes were too low-cut for my body. Week after week I would have long conversations with Randall Christensen, the show's lead costumer, about how I thought the costumes should look. I didn't want to show my stomach. I didn't want the back of a gown to expose my entire back, right to the top of my rear end. I didn't like seeing that much Cheryl on TV.

But Randall (God bless him) believed that I needed to celebrate my body more. He complimented my curves with some of the most amazing outfits on the show. "Honey, trust me. You're going to look great!" he said, trying to bolster my confidence. "Do you know how many women out there would die to have a figure like yours?"

I didn't believe him. I couldn't believe him. To believe him went against everything I'd ever thought about myself. Never in a thousand years did I think that women would envy my figure. I wasn't comfortable in my own skin, so why would anybody else be? I looked around at the other female dancers on our show, like Edyta Sliwinska. She has such an amazing, well-proportioned body. I would have died to have legs like hers. A couple of seasons later an Australian dancer named Kym Johnson joined the show. She was tall, blond, and blue-eyed—in a word, gorgeous. Standing next to Edyta and Kym I felt short, squat, and dumpy.

During the summer of 2008, in between seasons six and seven of the show, I took a vacation. I was exhausted. My season six partner, Cristian de la Fuente, and I made it all the way to the finals, but his arm injury greatly complicated things. He had only one arm to dance with and to lead with.

It's an absolutely incredible feeling to make it to the finals of *Dancing with the Stars*, but there's hardly any time for celebration. When you make it to that point on the show, you've been rehearsing with your partner for an average of four hours a day, six days a week, for the past fourteen to sixteen weeks—and each week you have one dance, or sometimes two dances, to learn. In the weeks that you have two dances, you increase your studio time from four hours a day to six.

When you make it to the season finale, you have to learn four dances in a week. That's not easy even for us pro dancers. It's very intense, and we end up increasing our rehearsals to eight to ten hours a day. And, of course, we have the show's camera crews following us, interviewing us about the different dances. Even though that lasts for only one week, it seems like a year, what with having to choreograph, teach, and rehearse four dances in five days.

The finals are a nice place to be, as a competitor, but I was exhausted. I had been dancing on the show for five consecutive seasons, not to mention dancing on tour during most of the off-seasons. I barely had any time to myself.

That summer I went on vacation with my family, then I traveled with a few friends to visit Cristian in his native Chile. We explored by day, ate incredible meals, and drank amazing Chilean wine at night. It was a wonderful trip.

When I got home I socialized with my friends for the first time in a long time. I went to the beach, walked along the shore, and relaxed. I even gained a few pounds, because for the first time in years, I wasn't dancing five or six hours a day, six days a week.

Star magazine ran a paparazzi photo of me walking on the beach in Malibu, wearing a bikini and sunglasses and having a good time. They printed it alongside a photo of me dancing when I was at my thinnest and made fun of me for having gained weight. It was just a couple of weeks before we were heading back for season seven of the show.

I knew that I had gained weight. I didn't know exactly how much, but I also knew that once I started dancing again I'd drop the weight. What I didn't know was that people would notice in such a big and cruel way.

My season seven partner was Olympic champion Maurice Greene, the nicest, most positive guy on the planet. He is someone who wakes up smiling—I'm convinced that he doesn't know any other way to be. It was fortunate for me to be around someone so optimistic during this time. When we were fitted for our costumes, I didn't feel as comfortable in them. I was a fuller version of my same size. My costumes still fit, but they were snug.

Maurice and I got ready for premiere night, and I was more than a little self-conscious. Nobody at the show said anything about my weight. Nobody even remotely acknowledged the *Star* magazine story. Nevertheless, in the back of my mind I wondered if anyone would notice that I had gained weight.

We performed two dances that night: the fox-trot and the mambo. The audience was as heavenly as always. We received solid scores for our first night out. I felt pretty good after the show, knowing that we'd done a great job.

The next morning was a completely different story. I turned on my computer to check my e-mail and look at some Web sites. Out of curiosity, I looked to see what the fans thought of the first night of the show. The comments outraged me. They said nothing about our dancing. Instead, the message boards were full of snide and downright cruel comments about my weight.

One person wrote that I had "back fat." Another person called me a "fat pig." Someone else suggested that Jenny Craig should hire me as its next spokesperson. The mean-spirited nature of the comments had me in tears. I called Kym, sobbing.

"Cheryl, why are you looking at these Web sites?" she asked soothingly. "Why do you care what some stupid blogger thinks about you? You are a beautiful woman. Don't let this stuff get you down. It's not worth it."

We talked for a long time, and I knew deep down that she was right. But I'm human. When someone says something mean, it hurts. I didn't want to leave the house.

Maurice was also supportive. "You know that the people who write these things are lonely and have nothing better to do than pick away at things, right?" he asked me at rehearsal. The more he tried to reason with me, the more I felt upset. I was hurt, embarrassed, and angry.

After the second week of the show that season, the mean-spirited comments continued, and I couldn't hide my frustration. I had gained some weight over the summer, but I was in no way out of control; yet some people acted as if I'd committed a crime.

I called my mom and my sister, and they tried their best to calm me down, too. "Cheryl, you gained a little weight, and people have noticed. Big deal," Mom said. "You're back to dancing every day again, and the weight will come off, and that will be that."

My mom was so matter-of-fact about it all because she knew that's exactly what would happen, and it did. Within the first two weeks of rehearsals with Maurice, I dropped five pounds. The physical weight was falling off me, but emotionally I still felt the weight of the world's eyes on me.

When I walked to the studio, I thought that people were looking at me differently. When I ate lunch, I felt people staring at my face, my arms, and my thighs. When I stepped out onto the dance floor, I was sure that people weren't watching me dance, they were trying to see where I'd gained weight and how much. I usually couldn't wait to get to the studio to rehearse, but during this period, I dreaded going to work and performing in front of the cameras because I was so paranoid about how I looked.

The salsa was a challenge for Maurice and me, and partly because of me. That season started off with a lot of press attention focused on me gaining weight, and I became very self-conscious about how I looked on camera. I started to feel so self-conscious that it almost became debilitating. I couldn't focus on choreographing a dance to its fullest potential, because all of the snide remarks that people might make were rattling around in my brain.

Something that finally helped me to move past that was help from one of my former dance partners, Paul Barris. Paul and I competed for about a year together. He's a really great salsa dancer, so he kindly came to Los Angeles to help me with ideas for choreographing the dance for Maurice and me.

Paul and I worked through the routine. A lot of dancers on the show work on ideas for choreography with fellow dancers rather than their celebrity partners because the dancers already know how to dance, so there is no teaching involved. We don't even have to talk; we just feel the energy and move around the dance floor to map out the routine. Most of my celebrity partners have never had any dance training, Maurice included.

It helped tremendously for me to get Paul's input and participation so that I in turn could illustrate the dance to Maurice. Maurice loved the music—Robin Thicke's "Everything I Can't Have"—and that really helped him to keep up with the fast-paced footwork. The steps in the salsa aren't as complicated as the steps in other dances, and it's fun.

Come show night, Maurice was on fire! He was so jazzed about getting out on the ballroom floor for the live audience. He seemed to have had absolutely no preshow jitters that night. I wondered whether he might have so much adrenaline surging through his body that he'd get ahead of himself during the routine, but his timing was terrific. The audience cheered, and he fed off that energy, going all out and earning us a robust score of twenty-seven points out of thirty. That salsa dance in week five turned out to be our breakthrough performance on the show.

After that performance, I finally started to feel focused on doing my job again. I was so grateful to Paul for taking the time to help me find myself with the choreography. It allowed

Maurice and me to really show off our skills and gave Maurice a chance to let his gregarious and energetic personality shine. Just by taking the time to help me focus on the dance instead of being so wrapped up in what my detractors might say, Paul gave me the confidence boost I needed to start fighting back.

My publicist, Susan, told me that she'd been getting calls from the press about my weight gain. All of a sudden such a ridiculous item had become a matter of national concern in the entertainment world. I wanted to have her tell the reporters where they could all stick their stories. But what would that solve? It would just let the bloggers know that their jabs had gotten to me. What really burned me up was that people were saying I was "fat as a size four"—a size *four*! They were perpetuating the age-old message in Hollywood that you have to be super-thin to be beautiful.

No sane person thinks that a woman who is size four is overweight. I do have curves—women are supposed to have curves. I always have, and I always will. I will never be the skeletal supermodel of magazines and runways and, frankly, I'm a lot healthier because of it. When the gossip magazines fixated on my weight, I eventually moved past being hurt just for myself and became indignant for every woman out there who is perfectly normal yet fears that her body isn't beautiful.

I started to get angry for every fifteen-year-old girl who wants to try out for the cheerleading squad but is afraid because she worries she won't look good in the uniform. I wanted to fight back for every wife whose husband has told her that she has to lose weight or he won't love her anymore. I wanted to stick up for every woman who has ever starved herself in order to try to be something she thought she should be because that's what the fashion industry and the media dictate.

I decided to speak my mind to *People* magazine, because I wanted to turn what I initially thought was a negative into a positive. At the beginning I had been worried what people thought about me. I had fallen into the trap of believing that in order to be on television, you have to be emaciated. After a couple of weeks of mulling things over and talking to Susan, Kym, and my family, I knew that I needed to make sure that I sent out the right message: I am proud of my curves.

My curves represent my mother, my aunts, and my grand-mother. They are part of what makes me unique. It took a long time for me to embrace that notion. But it's true. Curvy women in the entertainment industry are constantly teased about their voluptuous figures. Women like Jennifer Lopez and Kim Kardashian are mocked all the time, which is ridiculous. These are gorgeous, shapely women. Tyra Banks and Jennifer Love Hewitt were both blasted for enjoying themselves on their beach vacations. Paparazzi photographed them looking like real women in their swimsuits, and the tabloids and bloggers poked fun. How awful is it in our society that women just can't enjoy life without constantly worrying at every turn, "Will someone think I look fat?" The day after the *People* article ran, I did an interview with Diane Sawyer on *Good Morning America* addressing these concerns. I was ready to face head-on the challenge from the tabloids and defend the obvious truth that women should celebrate their bodies, not hate and abuse them.

About that same time, a *TV Guide* reporter questioned my fellow pro dancers Maksim Chmerkovskiy and Louis van Amstel; they said that I needed to watch my weight. They thought that people look to dancers as having "to die for" bodies. What kind of example was I setting by gaining weight?

Celebrate your curves.

Those comments made things a little tense behind the scenes for a while. I was hurt that Maksim and Louis didn't seem to have my back; they were upset that their comments were taken too "literally" and supposedly out of context. In the end, we all took the high road and moved on. After all, we were going to see one another all season. I had to let go of any anger so that I could keep moving forward.

But that's not to say that I didn't hold on to the glaring truth of the whole ugly incident. I had to face the fact that my body and my metabolism were changing. I was getting older. I was only twenty-four years old at the time, but my body was no longer responding to big dinners or nights out the way it used to.

I started making changes in my diet. I cut way down on carbs. I was dedicated to eating well again: no fried foods, no cooking with butter or oils, no eating out every night at restaurants. Instead of going to the craft services table at work, which is loaded with cookies, candy, and chips and salsa, I packed some hummus and carrot sticks or string cheese and fruit in my bag. I started drinking more water every day and going to bed at a decent hour every night.

Now it's extremely rare that I ever go a day without breaking a sweat. Even when I'm on vacation, I absolutely have to get some form of exercise—the treadmill, a jazzercise class, tennis—in addition to dancing every day.

I used to say that the scale was not my friend. He (I'm convinced that scales are male) is not kind. But he is in my bathroom, and I step on him every morning. I know what I need to weigh in order to feel good about myself and look good. Yes, I said it: I need to look good. I am on television, and as long as I am on *Dancing with the Stars* I will make sure that I look the part. I used to dread going to the gym or doing any type of repetitive cardio training, but now I love it. It's my personal responsibility and has become as much a part of my daily routine as brushing my teeth.

I've noticed residual benefits from my new lifestyle, too. I'm stronger physically and mentally, I sleep better, and I am more present in my day-to-day life. I have more energy and more patience. I am a better me than I've ever been in my life.

That's not to say that I still don't have moments of wishful thinking. Many of us do, and I think it's normal. I still wish that my legs were longer. Oh, to be just three or four inches taller (I'm five feet four) would be, I imagine, so delightful. But that's not going to happen, and that's okay. I've arrived at a peaceful place with all of this because I have gotten positive feedback from lots of fans.

RUMBA TIP

You need to be flexible, sexy, and sensual with your partner. Focus on good hip action. You move much more slowly than in the salsa, but movement is key.

At first people came up to me and in a hushed, defensive tone said, "You are so not fat. We love you exactly the way you are!" Nowadays, people are a bit less shy. "You look amazing. You go, Cheryl!" they say, often eager to give me a hug. It's an amazing feeling. I can honestly say that I'm happy and very much at ease with who I am and how I feel. And that's what matters most.

THE QUICKSTEP

Branching Out

7

The quickstep features both slow and very quick foot movements. The dance combines speed with an exceptionally sophisticated, refined manner. Although it appears to be similar in nature to the fox-trot, the quickstep, which was developed in England, has very distinctive movements. It's one of the more advanced ballroom dances because of its brisk pace and complex steps. The dancers should appear to be walking on a cloud, their feet barely touching the ballroom floor. All the while, elegance is key. The male partner usually wears a tuxedo with tails, and the female partner wears a conservative, long, flowing gown. The duo must maintain a firm body posture throughout the routine.

The quickstep is very much like the kind of atmosphere in which I was raised. As a young girl, I watched my mother work constantly at building her nursing business, Nurse Providers. She was always on the go, from the time I got up until long after I went to bed. I have many memories of my mom talking on the phone at home, conducting meetings in her office, and taking calls on her cell phone while I was at a dance lesson. She was always going, going, going, in a way that left me a little breathless.

I didn't understand it as a kid. I wanted my mom to watch television with me. I wanted my mom to tuck me in every night. I didn't understand why I couldn't have her all of the time. My nanny, Ima, used to tell me that my mother worked hard so that she could provide a nice life for our family.

"You mother loves you so much, and she doesn't want you or your sister to have to worry whether you're going to have a good meal to eat for dinner," Ima would say to try to soothe me. "Life in the Philippines can be hard. But you live in America, and your mother is working hard so that you can live the American dream."

I wasn't sure what it meant, but it sounded great: the American dream. I asked my mom about it one night when I was about ten. She explained to me that the phrase derived from immigrants who came to the United States in the hope of having a better life than they had had in their native countries.

I learned about Ellis Island in school. People came to the United States by boat from all over the world in order to start over. They wanted to educate their children in American schools. They wanted to build their businesses in this country. They knew that if they worked hard, they could make their dreams come true. Those dreams were very simple, my mother told me, and they were the very same dreams that she had for our family.

"People want to be able to put food on the table and provide a nice place for their families to live," she explained. "When I grew up in the Philippines, it was very difficult to earn a decent living. It was such a struggle for your grandmother and grandfather to pay the bills and feed me and all of my brothers and sisters. They encouraged me to come to America because they wanted me to be exposed to opportunities that just don't exist in the Philippines."

It was one of the first heart-to-heart conversations I ever had with my mother. I was so young that I didn't understand fully at the time what she was trying to explain to me. But her words and her story stuck with me. I began to relate to her in an entirely different manner after that point. Instead of resenting that she couldn't spend more time with me, I became more understanding that she was working hard, because her business was her passion, and the promise that it provided was her dream for all of us.

She wanted the best for her family, and she worked hard to earn money so that we could take the dance lessons we wanted to take or go on great family vacations every year. I think her drive was also fueled by the fact that she and my father had divorced when I was so young. What ultimately pushed her to be a successful businesswoman was that she didn't want to have to rely on someone else to provide for her. She didn't want to ask anybody to do favors for her or cut her some slack. She craved the confidence and pride that self-sufficiency brought her. That's the philosophy I was raised with.

Maybe this is why I don't get fazed when the dreaded quickstep comes around on *Dancing with the Stars*. During my childhood, my mother kept me moving, stepping, kicking, and hopping—and all at a pace that would have left anyone else dizzy.

When you find something you're passionate about, pursue it with confidence.

It's funny when I think about all of the partners I've had on *Dancing with the Stars*. At the beginning of the season they all say to me, "Cheryl, you're the expert" or "Whatever you say, Cheryl." But as the weeks go by, the tables often turn, ever so slightly.

I can't help but giggle when I think of the seasons when I danced with actors Cristian de la Fuente and Gilles Marini. Both of these men are the epitome of masculinity, exuding passion and sex appeal. When we did the tango, Gilles seemed to channel the intensity of the dance right through his veins. "I got this one, baby. I am French. I can do this," he purred.

He did. He interpreted the tango with a seriousness that translated onto the ballroom floor like a steamy scene from a Hollywood movie. He was able to get into the character of the dance, and we scored very well. In fact, it was only the fourth week of competition when Gilles and I danced the Argentine tango and received our first perfect score of the season. After our performance, one of the judges, Carrie Ann Inaba, remarked that she couldn't tell which of us was the professional dancer. That was a huge compliment for Gilles and a pretty good boost for me, too. After all, a dancer's goal should always be to make the partner look good.

The men I've worked with have generally had no problem getting into the passion of the tango, but things don't always fall into place as easily with the quickstep. Both Gilles and Cristian were athletic and coordinated, which is tremendously helpful for doing the quickstep, but they were challenged with the pace. The quickstep is fast, fast, fast; hop, hop, hop; jump and kick and jump and kick, then run across the floor.

All of this fancy, fast-paced footwork is done while the couple is in a close hold. There's no time to be looking at your feet, counting steps, or taking things slowly. This is a dance for which you have to jump in and just start going. At times the footwork is like a combination of hopscotch and soccer. In fact, I tried to appeal to the guys' soccer backgrounds, since both of them knew what it was like to be in the middle of a cluster of players going after the ball.

I told Gilles, "When you're playing soccer, and three other guys and you are trying to kick the ball out into the open, the last thing you want to do is get kicked in the shins, right?"

He nodded.

"So think of the quickstep in that regard. You have to have quick footwork like you do in a soccer match," I said, showing him that when I kicked my foot out, he should jump and spread his legs wide enough so that I didn't kick him in the shins. Then when he kicked his leg out, I spread my legs wide enough so that he didn't kick me in the shins.

We put on the music, which was 3 Doors Down's "Kryptonite," and I launched right into the dance.

"Wait! Wait! Wait!" he hollered, slightly panicked. "We need to do this a little slower."

"This isn't a slow dance," I explained.

"Cheryl, I just need to see what you're doing."

"But you can't look down. There's no looking down. You have to go, go, go. There's no time to think."

We went at it again. And again. And again. All week we tirelessly hoofed our way through the dance. We both took a few kicks in the shin and had a few choice words to say, which I'm sure were bleeped out by the production crew. The next time this dance comes around on the show, I've got to remember to invest in shin guards. It's for my partner's protection—and my own!

When show night arrived, Gilles was not feeling 100 percent great about the routine. He thought that he had the footwork down, but at the end of the dance he was supposed to slide on his knees toward the camera and rip open his shirt to reveal a Supermanlike *S* on his shirt. For legal reasons, we couldn't use the real Superman logo, so we did a *Dancing* designer version of it. For some reason, Gilles thought that it was going to make him look feminine. He called me the night before the performance show and suggested that we nix the last move.

"Relax," I reassured him. "People are going to love it. It's our big finish."

Sure enough, we got a great score for our quickstep: twenty-seven points out of thirty. Not bad at all. The judges were especially impressed with the routine. Len said he thought that Gilles was going to be a one-week wonder, and he was happy to see that his instinct was wrong. Indeed, Gilles proved he could do ballroom and Latin dancing very well. The funniest thing of all is that people still comment on that quickstep to this day, and it's all because of the move in which Gilles ripped open his shirt to become Superman.

As for Cristian and me—well, we tried. We did the quickstep during the second week of the show but I'm sad to say that we didn't fare as well in the critique and scoring. In fact, it was so hectic and sloppy that Carrie Ann actually called the routine "a mess." Len hated it, too. He thought it was too spastic. We got a painfully low score of twenty points out of thirty. Yikes.

In our defense, I must add that the quickstep is really hard to do in week two. We had been rehearsing together only a short time at that point, and the complexity of the footwork makes it one of the most difficult ballroom dances there is.

It's a lot to teach somebody early in the show; it's a dance that people usually get the hang of a little more quickly once they have some dance experience under their belts. You also have to take into consideration the height difference between Cristian and me—I'm five feet four and he's six feet two—which definitely took some getting used to. If we could have done that dance in week eight instead of week two, I have no doubt that we would have given a much better performance. I am thankful, though, that the fans voted us through, and the following week we redeemed ourselves by performing a respectable jive routine.

You win some, you lose some. But just as I inherently knew that Gilles's Superman finish would be a showstopper, my mother knew what I was capable of, and she also knew the dance of life well enough to understand just what I needed to do to realize that potential.

☆ ☆ ☆

My dance career had been steadily growing, but it really took off when I landed on *Dancing with the Stars* in 2006, and it was then that my mother pounced on the opportunity to educate me on the finer points of building a brand. I was making a decent amount of money for the first time in my life, and Mom did not want to see me squander it by living for the moment instead of with a sense of responsibility. That meant buying a nice car, but not a lavish one. It meant making sound investments and planning for my future. It meant building on my current opportunity by creating something even greater.

It was difficult for me to think about my future when I was twenty-one years old. I resisted my mom's input for a while because I just didn't get it. I didn't understand why she was telling me to think three, five, or ten years ahead. Why couldn't I just enjoy my life the way it was? I was living in a great city, making a good living doing what I loved, and supporting myself entirely for the first time ever. I was having a great time being a young, successful woman.

My mom could see that, and she was happy for me. She knew that she didn't have to parent me, per se, any longer, but her outlook on life was the epitome of the quickstep: she knew that I couldn't slow down to look at my feet or count my steps. I still needed some guidance every now and then if I was going to maximize my potential.

"You want to be your own woman and be independent, but you need to start thinking about a plan B," my mom gently explained. She had talked in the past about having a plan B and a plan C—and even a plan D. I needed to keep thinking about tomorrow and the next day and the next day, she told me. My mom was always thinking about what was next for me. What if I broke my leg? What would happen to me if I couldn't dance anymore?

Living in the moment is closing your eyes to the uncertainty of life.

Thanks to my mom's constant reminders, I started thinking about branding and building on the success I'd achieved from

Dancing with the Stars by forging ahead with opening a dance studio. I like to think that I would have done it on my own, but the truth is that I probably wouldn't have. I just didn't have the knowledge of how to go about starting my own business. Some people would be cautious about going into business with a family member, but I can't think of anyone I trust more than my mother. She has an MBA and is incredibly savvy at making sound decisions. Most of all, she's got my best interests at heart. She had already sold her company and was ready to help me start building and running mine.

We had a few meetings about a studio space that was available in the Potrero Hill area of San Francisco. That was a perfect place for my first studio, because it was not too far from where my parents live. I would never have the time to run and operate the studio from Los Angeles, so my mom agreed to get things off the ground for me. She insisted that the studio, which was originally called Metronome Dance Center, be named after me, but that made me feel a little squeamish.

"We need to call it Cheryl Burke's or Cheryl Burke Dance Center or Cheryl Burke Dance Studio," my mom said to me one day as we were brainstorming what to name the studio.

I shook my head. "I don't know about my name being the name of the studio. That feels weird to me."

"Don't be ridiculous," she said, in her usual no-nonsense, business-tycoon voice. "That is the whole point of building your brand."

It still felt odd, though—uncomfortable and egotistical. Why would somebody want to go to a dance studio with my name on it? I resisted, but my mom was insistent, and so were my agent and my publicist. They all thought it was a no-brainer to put my name on the building.

We ultimately settled on Cheryl Burke Dance as the name, and we decided to offer as many different styles as possible. Although I'm known for my ballroom dancing, we didn't want to limit the types of classes people could take. What if a bride wanted to learn how to dance for her wedding? What if a couple wanted to dance at their anniversary party? What if a child wanted to learn hip-hop? We wanted to make sure that students could choose from a wide range of styles that would bring people to whatever form of dance appealed to them.

Once our game plan was in place, we started slowly expanding the class schedule. We hired some amazing dance instructors and put together our first Cheryl Burke Dance team. I couldn't believe it was all coming together: The plan, the vision, the pie-in-the-sky dream was about to become a reality.

We decided to have our grand opening celebration on April 4, 2008. My publicist spread the word to photographers and media outlets around San Francisco. My season two partner, Drew Lachey, and my season six partner, Cristian de la Fuente, both flew up to be there. *Dancing's* host, Tom Bergeron, also made the trek, which truly touched me. Together they all helped my family and me to open the Potrero Hill studio in grand style. My mother was beaming as fans of all ages lined the street and many more people gathered outside to help us celebrate and wish us well. It was truly extraordinary. I could not believe the outpouring of support we received that night.

With that studio open and operating, we began looking at other locations in order to open a second studio. I have to give credit to my mother for keeping the ball rolling. The woman has incredible drive, which is something I didn't understand when I was a child, but I really appreciate it now. I also understand now why my mom encouraged me to go to college. "I wish you would have taken more business courses, Cheryl. Then I wouldn't have to teach you everything step by step," my mom groaned to me time and again.

What can I say? You can't have it all. If I had stayed in college, where I was extremely unhappy, I wouldn't have been able to pursue the unique opportunities that dance has brought my way. So maybe now I'm a little behind the curve in calling all the shots for my business, but my mom is the best teacher I can imagine to help me catch up.

At about the same time that we explored expanding my dance studios, I became friends with Kristi Yamaguchi, an Olympic figure skating champion and one of the most recognizable faces in sports. She's also created a solid brand for herself in the past decade. Kristi was a contestant on season six of *Dancing with the Stars*, and she introduced me to her sports agent, Yuki Saegusa. Yuki works with IMG (International Marketing Group), which is arguably the leading sports management company in the world. In addition to Kristi, some of IMG's most recognizable clients include football star Peyton Manning, race-car driver Danica Patrick, and models Gisele

Bundchen and Heidi Klum. IMG helps its clients develop their respective brands through licensing and endorsements, and that's just what I was looking to do.

Yuki came to some of the shows to see Kristi and her partner, Mark Ballas, perform. While she was there, we talked about my vision of opening more dance studios and taking my career to the next level. Yuki invited me to meet with her and her associates the next time I was in New York City.

A few weeks later, I was strolling down the streets of Manhattan to the IMG office. As I walked through the doors, it hit me: a huge picture of Tiger Woods, one of IMG's biggest clients, hanging in the lobby. At that time he was the king of the athletic world, and every company wanted him to endorse its products. "I want to be the Tiger Woods of the ballroom dance world," I declared to Yuki.

She smiled. "That is why we are here, Cheryl. We see great potential, because you are very popular with television viewers, especially the key female demographic." She had market research that showed that women in the eighteen to forty-nine age bracket responded very positively to my image. Yuki outlined what she and her company could do to help me expand my career; she explained how endorsement deals work, what kinds of personal appearances I might make, how to cross-market, and how I could even work my way into some broadcasting opportunities.

It was an exciting meeting for me, but it forced me to reconsider my image. I had only ever seen myself as a dancer, but now, as I was looking to the future and all of the opportunities ahead of me, I saw that I needed to take a long look at the life I was living as a single woman in Los Angeles. My social patterns changed a bit as I started focusing on developing my brand and the opportunities ahead of me. As I mentioned earlier, I had stopped going to clubs as often as I used to and started entertaining friends at home.

I knew that I had to do more to ensure that I was the kind of role model I wanted to be. I took a long look at what is and what isn't important to me. My family is my number one priority, and my career and my health are number two, since they go hand in hand. If I wanted to become a symbol of fitness and vitality, I needed to really focus on taking care of myself. That meant getting enough sleep, eating well, and exercising; these basic life necessities are all vital to my brand. I launched something of a personal-life makeover to be sure that my habits were all in line with what is truly important to me.

It wasn't long before Yuki came to me with a few offers to consider. We had decided that anything I endorsed I would have to believe in, and my first two endorsements were for products I loved.

One was with Crest Whitening Expressions; I appeared in a print ad for a contest that fans could enter to come up with a new catchphrase for the product. Since a dazzling white smile is very important in the overall polished, glamorous look for competitive ballroom dancing, that deal was a perfect fit for me.

The other was for the Sexy Hair product line (along with country singer Kellie Pickler). That endorsement also made sense for me because I was known for my distinctive hairstyles on the show, and people used to comment on how my hair moved with me when I danced. Once I started using Sexy Hair, I got many compliments on how shiny and healthy my hair looked. I loved being part of that ad campaign.

I also embarked on expanding my brand through dance instruction. Along with Maksim Chmerkovskiy, one of my fellow dancers from the show, I did an exercise dance DVD called *Dancing with the Stars: Latin Cardio Dance*. The DVD, released in September 2008, became popular right away because it made it easy for people to learn how to do basic Latin dance moves in the comfort of their own homes. Not long after the DVD was released, we got a lot of fan mail thanking us for such a fun video that not only taught people to dance but also helped them to lose weight or get their kids active on a rainy day. I was so thrilled to hear that I was helping people become healthy.

In 2009 I launched my own line of fitness wear for FitCouture.com. I enjoy working out in stretchy lycra fitness pants and tank tops, and I got a lot of requests from fans of *Dancing with the Stars* to design comfortable workout attire based on what I like to wear. I like long pants and matching jackets, and black is my favorite color, so that was the base from which I started before adding accent colors and pockets.

The jacket had to have pockets. That was a big complaint of mine about other brands of exercise wear. Where is a dancer supposed to stash her car keys or cell phone when she runs into Starbucks or stops to fill her car with gas on the way home from the studio? I also wanted to make sure that the pants had a flare at the bottom—just enough to give the illusion of elongating the leg. I made sure that the clothing was something that a woman could wear to the gym or to the grocery store and feel confident that she looked great, even though she was just wearing workout clothes.

The first day that the clothing was available for consumers to purchase on FitCouture.com, the Web site crashed. It was disappointing that everyone couldn't order the product right away, but I was so excited that I was designing fitness attire that women really wanted to wear. I created a new line for 2010, and I can't wait to get started on a 2011 line.

I opened two more dance studios at the end of 2009, and I signed a deal to start franchising the studios around the country. My mom and I joke about how I am working my way through the alphabet with all of the different directions in which I've been able to expand my career. Plan A was joining *Dancing with the Stars*. Plan B was opening the first dance studio. Plan C was the fitness DVDs and the endorsement deals. Plan D was the clothing line. Plan E is franchising the dance studios, which should mean more locations by the end of 2011.

Plan F is to launch a Cheryl Burke–branded show in Las Vegas in the next few years. My dream is that an experienced choreographer and director will want to partner with me so that we can have a feature show at one of the hotels on the Las Vegas Strip. I have even talked to Celine Dion about it— she's a huge fan of *Dancing with the Stars*. I also have my dear friend and former *Dancing* partner Wayne Newton to talk to for ideas. He's an absolute icon in Sin City, and he knows what elements a show needs to have to be a success. My fingers are

QUICKSTEP TIP

This is a high-energy dance in which the partners must keep holding on to each other. You have to be light on your feet and move around the floor as a unit. And don't forget to smile.

crossed that the next few years will bring me the opportunities I'm working toward.

I know that all this seems like a lot to tackle, but I like being busy. I'm always thinking now about what is next. I do enjoy being in the moment, but I'm so used to being active, physically and mentally, that it's hard to not jump back into planning mode after a while. When I took college courses at age eighteen, I wasn't motivated to learn, because the subject matter didn't excite me. But now that my work and business ventures go hand in hand, I'm absolutely motivated—and I have no plans to slow down anytime soon.

8

THE VIENNESE WALTZ

Grace under Pressure

The Viennese waltz is an enchanting formal dance that flows so gently and seamlessly that the dancers appear to be floating on air. This is believed to be the oldest and most traditional of all the ballroom dances, originating in Austria in the late 1700s. Following the etiquette, the male partner dons a tuxedo with tails while the female partner wears a long ballgown. Together, in a formal hold, the partners continually turn clockwise and counterclockwise as they navigate the ballroom floor.

Every time I teach one of my celebrity partners the Viennese waltz, we usually agree on the wardrobe. Men get to look suave and debonair in a nice suit or tuxedo, and women wear a long, flowing gown and have their hair down. But we usually face a big challenge in the execution of the movements. Because the Viennese waltz is such an elegant formal dance, there are quite a few "do this but not that" instructions that go along with it.

With Drew Lachey in season two, I had to help him keep his shoulders down and his chin up. He struggled to keep his frame in the correct position as he held me in the very formal pose. He also had trouble with not being able to look at me while we danced. The Viennese waltz has an element of arrogance mixed in with its beauty: the partners hold their heads back and their arms extended.

Then there's the spinning. Picture a music box with a tiny couple that spins around as the music plays. In the Viennese waltz, the couple must spin the same way, moving about the floor while holding each other firmly but not gazing at each other. It is very important to maintain the smooth rhythm by not making the arm movements too jerky.

Gilles Marini had a tremendous time trying to master his arm movements during season eight. He was used to the sharpness that the Latin dances required, so it was difficult for him to transition to slower, more fluid moves. I told him to try to imagine himself in the deep end of a pool, trying to swim his way to the surface. The resistance he would feel as he stroked his way through the water would slow him down—that was how his movements should look when dancing the Viennese waltz.

To really drive home what I was telling him, we spent a few hours during rehearsal at a pool with a synchronized swimmer. Gilles got into an old-fashioned, one-piece, zip-up bathing suit. It was a sight to see, and it was all caught on tape by our fabulous production team.

Arm technique aside, probably the most challenging aspect of this dance is the constant movement and spinning around. I can't tell you how many times I've heard my partners struggle with the dizzying effect of the Viennese waltz. For a beginner, it's a lot like the spinning teacup ride at Disneyland.

"Hold on, you're going too fast," Maurice Greene told me.

"Really? I'm going too fast for an Olympic gold medal track star?" I joked.

"Seriously, girl. This is making me dizzy," he said, holding his head.

I heard the same thing from Drew and from Gilles. The waltz looks a lot easier than it actually is, but people also psych themselves out by overthinking every little aspect. The key to doing this dance well is to hold on to your partner and then put yourself on cruise control. Just enjoy the ride. I've given this advice to all of my partners over the years, and it's worked every time.

✫ ☆ ✫

The Viennese waltz is kind of a metaphor for my life these days. I hold on tightly and maintain control of where I'm going and what I'm doing. But I also have the ability to let go and enjoy the ride along the way.

The control comes into play with my work and making decisions about my business life. When I moved to Los Angeles, I was happy just to be earning a paycheck to support myself. I didn't look too far ahead to think about what might become of my role on a television show. But as the show grew and became more popular, so did my understanding of the impact it was making.

The show has sparked many wonderful things for me. It helped me to realize my dream of owning my own dance studios. It also brought me tremendous opportunities in the entertainment business. I've traveled all around the world to perform. I've hosted events and have done on-camera interviews. I've also been presented with a variety of endorsement deals. That's all wonderful, but money isn't everything. What's more important to me is being fulfilled by what I do.

Throughout the years I have become fulfilled in many richer, deeper ways than I ever imagined. I love to dance and please a crowd. But as I've gotten older, I've become more appreciative of the fans of our show. It might sound corny, but I've met some of the most extraordinary people throughout the years, and they have affected me very deeply.

In the early days on *Dancing with the Stars*, I was often in an airport waiting to board a plane, and occasionally a person came up to me and asked, "Are you Cheryl Burke? I just love you! May I have a picture?" Those early encounters with fans were always sweet and positive. But I can remember thinking, "Oh, no! I didn't wear any makeup today. I look awful. Oh, well. At least they like me!"

Around the middle of my second season, when I was dancing with Emmitt Smith, I started to get fan mail. The early
fan mail was incredible. People were so kind, complimenting
me on how well they thought I was doing on the show. "I
voted for you on my cell phone, my mother's cell phone, my
computer, and my home phone," some of the messages read.
I was so tickled by the sweet support and encouragement that
people sent.

Then one day I received a note from the parents of a young
girl in the Chicago area who was very ill with leukemia. I was
going to be in Chicago to appear on *Oprah*, and my mom and I
agreed that it would be a tremendous boost for this girl's spirits
if I went to the hospital to visit her. We made arrangements
with her parents to surprise her, and after taping with Oprah, I
headed over to the hospital.

"Oh, my gosh. It's really you!" the little girl squealed as she
sat up in bed. "I have been dreaming of meeting you!"

"You have?" I asked, incredulous that someone would be
so excited to meet me. "I've heard a lot about you," I told her.
"You want to be a dancer someday, right?" She nodded. "Then
you're going to need a good pair of dancing shoes."

I pulled a pair of dancing shoes out of my bag and handed
them to her.

"I can really have these?" she asked, her eyes huge.

"Absolutely, sweetie," I told her, as I leaned over to give her
a big hug. It just about tore my heart out. I wanted to make her
better. I wanted to snap my fingers and, like that, have her up
and dancing as a ten-year-old girl should be. Instead, she was

hooked up to an IV, pale, and weak—except for her spirit. She was so positive and so full of enthusiasm. I was impressed with her strength and her will to fight the disease. She told me that she was going to put on the shoes and start dancing just as soon as she was better.

I wanted to spend more time with that remarkable little girl, but I had to get back to Los Angeles to do the show. I couldn't stop thinking about her, though. I almost felt guilty that perhaps I had gotten more out of our visit than she had.

I felt grateful for my health, for my life, and for having the ability and the opportunity to travel and do exciting things. Most of all, I felt grateful that this young child reached out to me. It was an honor to spend time with her.

Since then, I've had many wonderful encounters with fans of all ages. So many women have come up to me to tell me that I've inspired them. They say that they have taken up dancing again because of watching me on the show. Women have said that because of *Dancing with the Stars*, they have rekindled connections with their husbands by taking ballroom lessons together. Others tell me that because of the scrutiny I received for gaining weight in 2008, they have become proactive about getting healthy.

When mothers tell me that their daughters have gotten into dancing because of watching me, it's kind of a jolt to my system (in the very best way), because I realize that I'm really inspiring people. Dance is something I've done my whole life. It's a talent I have that I love to showcase and share with others, but to think that doing what I do has changed people's lives is a huge thing.

Nevertheless, I hate to admit it—and this is true for many people who are in the public eye—there are times I've taken my blessings for granted. After several seasons on the show, the excitement wore off and reality set in. Getting on and off airplanes, rehearsing and dancing on the show, and making personal appearances at events sometimes felt more like a chore than fun. I remember being invited to make an appearance at an event in Las Vegas for which my airfare, my hotel room, and all of my expenses and meals would be paid. All I had to do was show up, and I would receive a first-class weekend. Oh, and I could bring a guest along.

Somehow I found a way to be a little put off by it. I mulled things over in my head. "Do I really want to go? I'm not sure I feel like it."

I talked to my younger sister, who put things back in perspective for me. "Cheryl, are you crazy? That sounds amazing!"

"It does?" I asked.

"Yes! You get to do the coolest stuff. Who else gets invitations like that? Do it!" she pleaded.

I went and had a blast. I relaxed by the pool; I got dressed up and went to a party one night; I took some photos with people and mingled; I met up with some friends in town and we had a great dinner together. It was such a fun weekend, and I was really glad that my sister reminded me to be grateful for opportunities like this that come my way. It can be tiring sometimes, but it's something I should be excited about rather than dreading.

Nothing, however, has reminded me of the incredible opportunities in my life like the fan encounter I had in my seventh season. My mother, visionary that she is, had helped me to start my own Web site a few seasons earlier. It enabled fans to see what I was up to, where I was performing, how I was doing on the show, and where I'd be teaching dance classes off-season. One day, as Mom was helping me sift through the e-mails on my Web site while we chatted on the phone, we came across one from a woman in Ohio. She wrote that her husband, Gary, was suffering from pancreatic cancer and didn't have long to live. She said that he was in tremendous pain, but what brought him joy every week was watching *Dancing with the Stars* with her. It made them both happy to share that time together. Because his illness was progressing rapidly, Gary's wife's letter had a sense of urgency to it. One of the items on his "bucket list," she wrote, was to sit in the audience and see me perform. My mom and I were floored.

"Cheryl," my mom said to me, "we have to make this happen fast."

"Mom, are you sure he wants to meet me?" I asked, seriously wondering if maybe this was some kind of mistake. "Wouldn't he rather meet someone a little more exciting, like George Clooney or Brad Pitt?"

"No, Cheryl. This woman says the show is so special to him. They watch it every week."

"I will talk to ABC and see what we can do," I assured her.

I spoke to my producer, who talked to someone else, and we were able to arrange for Gary and his wife to fly out to Los Angeles, stay at a nearby hotel, and sit in the front row of the show.

I told Gilles, my partner at the time, about Gary, and Gilles was very moved. Gary's illness struck a chord with Gilles, whose father had died of the same disease when Gilles was a young man.

"Cheryl," Gilles told me, tears welling up in his eyes. "We have to make this the best night of his life. This is so incredible that all this man wants is a little escape from being sick. My father was so sick, and there was very little we could do to make him feel better. We are dancing for Gary on Monday night."

It was sheer determination that helped Gary get on the plane and fly to Los Angeles with his wife by his side. When they arrived, his wife confessed that she had been doubtful Gary would be able to make the trip, but that he had told her, "This is my favorite show. There's no way I'm not going."

I can honestly say that the people I work with at *Dancing with the Stars* are some of the most kindhearted folks I have ever met. They really rolled out the red carpet for Gary that night.

Gilles and I met Gary and his wife before the show, and they had brought me flowers. Gary was already having the time of his life; he had explored the backstage area, met some of the other dancers on the show, and then—at Gilles's insistence—been seated in the front row next to Carole, Gilles's wife. There was Gary, knowing that his time was short, holding his wife's hand as they shared this last big trip together.

Gilles and I performed, and after we finished, we both glanced over at Gary and winked. He was so happy. Carole told us after the show that Gary never stopped smiling throughout the entire show.

Afterward we all met up again and talked about having dinner together—Gary and his wife, Gilles and his wife, and my boyfriend and I. But Gary was feeling weak; he was perspiring heavily and felt dizzy. He had no strength, and he asked if he could bow out of dinner. Gilles recognized that the night was probably a bit overwhelming for Gary because his health was so fragile.

"You should go see a doctor, Gary," Gilles said softly. "I tell you, I will feel a lot better if you just get checked out and make sure you're doing well. We can have dinner another time. I want you to get some rest."

Gilles asked the driver of his car service to please take Gary and his wife to Cedars-Sinai Medical Center and to stay until they were ready to leave. The driver kindly obliged, and Gary, after meeting with a doctor, went back to his hotel for a few hours before he had to head to the airport to catch his flight home.

Gilles and I were broken up that night. We were frustrated that we couldn't do more for Gary. Taking photos, visiting with him before the show, and dancing our hearts out had made him very happy, and he was full of gratitude. But the next day, as I looked at the flowers he had given me, I felt helpless and frustrated. I wanted so much to be able to give health back to this kind, wonderful man.

In the months after his visit to Los Angeles, Gary's condition steadily worsened. Gilles kept in close touch with him, often talking on the phone with him and his wife. Gilles made sure that Gary knew that if he ever wanted to come back to Los Angeles, he had a friend waiting for him.

VIENNESE WALTZ TIP

You're constantly going in circles (try not to get dizzy!), and it's important to move gracefully around the floor. There's a rise and fall in the dance—going up and down in time to the music—and you're holding your partner very close.

In late 2009, Gary passed away. The last few months of Gary's life were like a Viennese waltz. He held on tightly as he battled for his health. But he also allowed himself to let go and enjoy his remaining days with his family. It broke our hearts to hear that he was gone.

That experience taught me something incredibly valuable. I learned that while our show is fun and frivolous, it also serves a very important purpose by putting a smile on people's faces. That's why every time I meet someone who wants to take a picture or talk for a moment, I thank him or her. I try to make sure that everyone takes away something very positive from an encounter with me.

Take time out for others, and you will be rewarded in kind.

This is what celebrity is really for. It's not about being able to afford expensive cars or go to swanky parties. It's about entertaining people, bringing them happiness, and making them feel good about themselves. If I can accomplish that with my work and in my daily life, then everything is worth it.

BEHIND THE SCENES

A Day in the Life at *Dancing with the Stars*

I can't tell you how many times fans ask me what it's like to be on *Dancing with the Stars*, but the answer is nothing I can sum up in a sentence or two. It's amazing. It's frustrating. It's exhilarating. It's exhausting. It's all of those things and then some—especially on the day of a live performance show.

All week long, starting on Tuesday, the couples on the show juggle rehearsals with wardrobe fittings, personal appearances, and family life. But none of those things quite compares to show day: Monday. For the rest of the world, Monday equals back-to-work day or drudgery. But at *Dancing with the Stars*, Monday is all about lights, cameras, sequins, and (in my case) spray tans.

It's true. Before I can do anything else on show day, I have to make sure that my tan is camera-ready, because my naturally pale skin can look washed out on screen. Sunday night, a good eighteen hours before our show goes live, I apply a layer of self-tanner all over my body. That night, before I go to bed, I pack my bag for the next day. I make sure that I have an outfit to change into after the show, as well as some magazines and my tanning lotion. I apply this lotion on Monday to enhance the Sunday night tan. Yes, I really am that pasty.

On Monday morning, I'm usually out the door by eight. I drive myself to the studio, groggy and in need of some strong coffee.

The women on the show are the first to arrive, because it takes us a lot longer to get ready. The pro and celebrity dancers take their turns in the makeup and hair trailers to get their fancy updos and glamorous faces put on. It's a blast. Music is playing, the women are talking about what they did over the weekend, and the producers pop in to make sure we're all moving along in a timely manner.

Melanie is the head makeup artist, and Mary is her counterpart for hair. Together they create the makeup and hair concepts that will coordinate best with our dances and our costumes. Days before show day, they go over to the wardrobe department and take pictures of people's costumes. Then they decide how we should have our hair and our makeup styled.

Through the years they have learned all of our quirks. Some women are self-conscious about having their hair up, whereas others don't like too much eye makeup. One of my quirks is that I will never wear bright red lipstick. I just don't like how that color looks on my lips. I am also self-conscious about my ears and my forehead—a holdover from childhood. I think that both of these features are too big and should be covered by my hair at all times, so when I have to have an updo, I always ask to have a piece of hair covering my ears. To minimize my forehead, I always wear bangs or swoop my hair off to the side to cover it up.

The girls in the trailer always used to roll their eyes. "Cheryl, you're crazy!" they said. "Your forehead is not huge!" But I know what I see when I see myself on camera, and nobody is ever going to be able to convince me to think otherwise. They do understand, however, that a woman moves best when she is confident about how she looks, so covering my forehead is not even a topic for discussion anymore.

I drink my coffee and eat a little something from the craft services table. The show serves breakfast and has everything from omelets and bacon to muffins, bagels, and fruit. I often ask the staff to whip up a breakfast burrito with egg whites, tomatoes, and salsa. That way I can get a lot of protein and flavor without a lot of calories. I also grab a little bowl of fruit to snack on throughout the morning.

By about eleven, we start taking turns doing what's called a band rehearsal with our partners. Most of us have our makeup almost all done, but our hair is still in rollers. We are also still wearing sweatpants or shorts and a tank top as we make our way to the main stage. This is the first time in the week that we rehearse on the show's ballroom floor with the full band.

All week long we've practiced with the CD version of the song we're dancing to. When we go in to rehearse with the live band, the song sounds different, so we sometimes need to make some small adjustments. Sometimes the tempo is a little bit different from what we've rehearsed to all week. This is generally something that the celebrity dancers have more difficulty adjusting to, so we do a run-through with the band two or three times to get used to it so they can feel more at ease about the live performance.

At this point my hair is usually falling out of its hairpins and only one of my false eyelash pieces is still on. I'm sure I look a little crazy, but none of us is quite show-ready just yet. Nevertheless, the cameras are rolling. As we rehearse with the band, the production crew makes sure that the cameras are in the right positions to capture our performance from various angles.

Through the years, I've become a bit nitpicky about how my partner and I look on camera. As much as we focus on technique and performance during rehearsal, I never get to see things from the television audience's perspective until the morning of the show—and then I snap into action. I have the production assistant who works with me film the monitor as my partner and I do the rehearsal. The assistant focuses my flip camera on the director's monitor, and that way I can see every camera angle and camera change just as the audience will see it at home. This also enables me to see where I might need to make some adjustments in our routine to improve it. Other pros do this, too, and it helps us to give our best possible performance.

Around noon, after band rehearsal, we go back into hair and makeup. We're hot and sweaty, so everything has to be touched up. It's also lunchtime, so you'll often see us grabbing food in a take-out container as we head back to the hair and makeup trailers.

One of the things people want to know is what I eat on show day and, more important, how I can eat at all when I have to wear such snug and often revealing costumes. Well, I can assure you that I don't indulge in a burger and fries on show day! I generally eat lightly and leanly the day before a show and the day of the show. My favorite meal is grilled chicken, steamed vegetables, and a small Caesar salad. Other dancers go for fruit, pasta, or rice, but I prefer to stick with what I know works best for me. I eat this very basic, simple meal that is nourishing but that also won't make me feel bloated or bogged down for the dress rehearsal or the show.

There's really no stopping the process on a Monday. No sooner do we eat—in between getting our hair done and our makeup touched up—than it's time to head to dress rehearsal. There's a body makeup artist who does touch-ups on me while I get dressed. I don't worry if my hair and my makeup aren't done at that point. For me, it's all about making sure that the tan is perfect. I can't go out in front of the cameras half tan and half not, or with big blotches where I've applied the lotion unevenly. I have to have total coverage, and the woman who has taken such great care of tanning me up is named Nadejh. She knows how picky I am, and, bless her, she takes the time to make sure I'm evenly bronzed from head to toe.

Once my tan is in place, I put on my dress and head over to my partner's trailer. We walk together to the main stage and take our places for the full dress rehearsal. At this time, all of the couples are in full hair, makeup, and costume.

The only difference between the full dress rehearsal and the live show (other than the rehearsal not being broadcast, of course) is that the judges do not watch the dress rehearsal. Instead, we have faux judges—people who look like our judges—who sit in Carrie Ann's, Len's, and Bruno's seats.

In the dress rehearsal, we run through the show from start to finish, even taking little pauses here and there for the scheduled commercial breaks. The theme music strikes up, and we are at the top of the staircase, just as we'd be at the start of the live show. Then we dance our routines, one by one. When we finish, we walk over to host Tom Bergeron to talk to the faux judges. They give us fake comments, and it's pretty funny because the comments are usually ridiculous, like: "I think your waltz was beautiful, but I'm not sure why you thought wearing rollers in your hair was a good idea" or "You guys look great together—and did you have the grilled salmon at lunch?" The goal is simply to fill the amount of time that the judges would have to critique us during the live telecast.

This is when the genius of Tom is on full display. If you like him on the live show, you should see him at our dress rehearsals. He likes to ad lib, and sometimes there's a lot of swearing and sarcastic humor that can make our dress rehearsals R-rated. It's all in great fun, because it loosens everyone up. As nervous as we all can be—and yes, we all get at least a little nervous before we perform—Tom keeps the atmosphere light by making us laugh. It's a nice reminder that even though we are putting on a live show as a competition, we're also there to entertain and have fun.

After dress rehearsal we have about an hour before the live show. That's when I usually go back to my trailer, take off my costume, and relax. Although the costumes are amazing to look at, some of them are not very comfortable to wear. The women joke that our dresses often have Wonder Woman–like bulletproof padding in the chest area. The dresses are usually skintight, with a little Lycra to move with us when we dance. They are nothing that you would want to lounge around in, especially if they have beads or sequins on them; you definitely don't want to sit on the delicate adornments, because that can damage them.

People often ask me if I get to keep any of my costumes. No, I am sad to say, I don't. The costumes belong to the show's lead costumer, Randall Christensen. He's a gem of a guy, and his designs have earned him an Emmy. When we do personal appearances, for example, whoever we perform for will rent the costume from Randall. Even though I don't have any show costumes at home in my closet, I do have my favorites. I love the "Save a Horse, Ride a Cowboy" outfit that I wore in season two when Drew Lachey and I did our freestyle routine.

Another favorite costume of mine is the green dress I wore when Emmitt Smith and I performed the samba (and won) on the season three finale.

As I wait for the show to begin, I slip into a robe and get final hair and makeup touch-ups. I also make sure to use the bathroom. I definitely don't want to worry about needing to do that during the show! And here is another of my little quirks: I never use the bathroom in my trailer because I am always terrified that the plumbing won't work. I always use the bathroom that is backstage instead.

During all of the final primping stages for the women, the men who are going to be on the show just hang out and relax. There may be less than an hour to go before we're live on the East Coast, but you'd never know it from the looks of Maksim Chmerkovskiy, Tony Dovolani, Mark Ballas, and Derek Hough. Those four are often hanging out, shirtless, playing football on the lot where our trailers are located. They run around like kids behind the studio and have a grand old time joking and playing catch. Sometimes Mark, who is an incredible musician, will play guitar in his trailer. The men can get dressed in about two minutes, so they are often tugging up their pants as we walk to the stage. It's hilarious.

Other people like to squeeze a power nap in between dress rehearsal and the live show, but not me. I tend to pace in my trailer, where I have a scented candle lit and music playing on my iPod, usually something like the Black Eyed Peas, Jay-Z, or Nero. I stretch a bit and try to relax before I have to put my costume back on and head to the stage with my partner. But

I am usually pretty tense. I can't help it—I'm a nervous wreck on Monday.

When the live show begins, it's a blur from start to finish. It goes so fast. In past seasons, when we weren't performing on stage, we sat in what is known as the Red Room. That room is off-camera, and it's where former cohost Samantha Harris interviewed us about our performance and awaited the judges' scores with us. For season ten, the producers thought it would be a great idea to relocate the Red Room to the dance floor. The room has glass walls, so the audience members can see in and we can see out. It's like living in a fishbowl or, as Tom so handily nicknamed it, "the Celebraquarium."

We are able to interact with one another and with the audience a bit more, and we can also enjoy the other performances live instead of watching them on a twenty-inch monitor. However, as one production staffer joked, "You're not going to be able to pick your noses!" So there's that. But we do have to be more mindful about how we sit or move so that we don't do anything inappropriate. Depending on when you are dancing on show night, your muscles can tighten up. It is sometimes a challenge to keep limber throughout the show, knowing that people are watching you do your stretching exercises.

When the live show is over, we do a gamut of press interviews with media outlets from around the country. The interviewers line up on the ballroom floor, and we make the rounds for about forty-five minutes, talking about the show, the judges' comments, the scores, and what our evening plans are.

Afterward, I go back to my trailer, change into my clothes, and go to dinner. Sometimes my family comes to town and we have dinner together; at other times, a group of us from the show will meet up for sushi or pasta. After that, we generally hit a club or two. The adrenaline that surges through your body on show day makes it hard to unwind—a lot like Christmas when you're a kid. I used to wake up on Christmas morning and could hardly wait to open the presents with my sister. Then we played and played until it was time to eat, but we were too excited to touch our dinner. Monday at *Dancing with the Stars* is a lot like that. It's a gift to be able to do what I do for a living. It never gets dull. It really doesn't.

My energy finally starts to fade sometime around one in the morning. That's when I head back to my house, pulling off my false eyelashes as I go. I really shouldn't admit this, but once or twice I tossed them out the window. So if you see any false eyelashes on Mulholland Drive, they're probably mine.

Once I get home, I take off my makeup with makeup wipes— just the simple kind you can buy at a drugstore. Then my head hits the pillow, and I sleep until about ten on Tuesday morning.

My mom flies into town every Monday to see the show, and she stays over at my house. So every Tuesday during the season, I know I can count on having a great breakfast. Mom makes sure that I have a good meal before I head back to the studio for the results show. Even though I'm a grown woman, I love having my mom mother me every now and then!

At the studio for the live results show, my partner and I, if we are lucky, will receive the good news that we're moving on to another week in the competition. Of course, when we get bad news instead and are eliminated, it's always a bittersweet feeling.

I think it's that way for all the dancers on the show. You try to ride the wave of the experience for as long as you can, but sometimes you can go only so far. I have had tremendous luck with my partners. The season with Tom DeLay was disappointing, because Tom suffered a foot injury and had to withdraw—something neither of us wanted—but we both knew it was the right decision for his health. But every other season, I have never felt that my time with my partner ended prematurely. Every time my partner and I have been voted off, it's been our time to go; it felt like it was the natural end of our journey together.

But if we live to see another week, there's no time to celebrate. After the hugs and high fives, I go straight back to my house and begin choreographing our next routine. There's no time to rest during a season of *Dancing with the Stars*. After I spend a few hours mapping out the dance in my head to the music we've been assigned, I get some sleep. Then it's back to rehearsal bright and early on Wednesday morning. The whole cycle starts over from there in the quest for the mirror ball trophy.

10

THANKS, PARTNERS

Partners for a Season, Lessons for a Lifetime

f there's one thing I've learned, it's that I will never stop learning. Even though I'm supposed to be the teacher on *Dancing with the Stars*, I have picked up quite a few lessons from my celebrity dance partners.

I came into the world of entertainment television young and green, wide-eyed and bewildered. At times it was exciting, new, and fun; at other times I was so overwhelmed that it knocked me off my feet. But through it all, I've managed to glean a few crucial pointers that have helped me to view my life and my world a little differently.

Two of my partners won the *Dancing with the Stars* trophy with me. But that doesn't make my other partners' efforts on the dance floor any less significant. They are all winners, and I'm fortunate to be able to call each of them my friend.

Drew Lachey: Be Yourself

When I look back at my first season (the show's second season), one of the things that makes me laugh—fondly—is how I adjusted slowly (and, at times, awkwardly) to being on television. I was so shy and kept wondering, "How am I going to do this?" Thank heavens for Drew Lachey.

The day I arrived in Los Angeles, a *Dancing with the Stars* camera crew and I made the trek to Drew's house to film our first meeting. I was wearing skinny jeans, a yellow tank top, and high heels in an effort to look like a glamorous, trendy, Hollywood fashionista. The field producer took one glance at what I was wearing and immediately told me that I'd have to change my shoes.

"It won't look good on camera if you are taller than Drew," the producer said. "Can you put on a pair of flats?"

At five feet, four inches, I've never been close to being tall, so it seemed weird to me that they thought my height in high heels would be a problem. I had purposely bought my jeans long so they would fit right with heels. I dug out a pair of

194

flip-flops from my luggage, and with my now too-long jeans dragging on the ground, we headed to Drew's house. The cameras were put into position, I rang the doorbell, and Drew opened the door. Although he's a few inches taller than me, I could almost look him in the eye; that was when I understood why the producer wanted me in flats. That was my first lesson in how the camera would rule my life.

I also learned that even though I might know quite a bit about teaching dance, I had a lot to learn about teaching someone one-to-one in front of a camera crew that was recording our every step and our entire conversation. I was extremely self-conscious when the cameras were around.

Drew and I hit it off from the start. I could tell right away that even though he was a very successful recording artist who had traveled the world and played in packed stadiums of screaming fans, he was very grounded. He and his home were so warm and inviting; there was nothing pretentious about him at all. He was not at all what I imagined a teen idol would be like. And, most important at that time, he was very in tune with how I was feeling; he could tell right away that I was a nervous wreck.

Drew was a natural in front of the cameras, whereas I became very quiet. How boring those early days of footage must have been for the crew! Drew knew that we needed good banter for the film segments, so he took the lead and kept the conversation going. The minute the crew left for the day, I felt the tension drain from my body, and then I was fine. In fact, I talked and joked back and forth with Drew, and we had a blast.

After a couple of days of this, Drew finally asked me, "Why aren't you like this when the cameras are on?"

"I'm afraid to make a mistake or sound like a dork, so I just don't say anything," I confessed.

"That's crazy." He laughed. "You're a great teacher, and you have a great sense of humor. You just need to relax and be yourself. Pretend they aren't even there."

"How do you do that in a dance studio where there are floor-to-ceiling mirrors on the walls?" I said, looking around.

"Just focus on me," Drew said. "When you're talking to me, look at me and ignore the crew."

So I did. When we rehearsed, Drew asked me questions that required more than a yes or no answer; soon, conversing back-and-forth became natural and easy. We were just two friends talking, not two people trying to put on a show for the cameras. Drew was right—if I just focused on talking to him, I was able to block the cameras out of my mind. Thanks to Drew's constant efforts at drawing me out of my shell, I was able to let my personality start to emerge while the camera crews were there. Sometimes a cameraman was just three feet away from us, but we kept on doing our thing because we focused on each other and not on the peripheral activity in the room.

Drew also taught me to become more comfortable with letting people see my personality in interviews. He kept telling me that press interviews could be fun.

"People love this show, and they love what you do. Have fun with it and just be yourself," he said. "Trust me, people will fall in love with who you are, not the person you think you need to be." Drew gave me pep talks before each interview, reminding me, "Be yourself. Be natural. Over time you'll get used to it."

He was right. I'm so much more at ease now in front of the cameras. In fact, my confidence level has risen so much that I even joined the ranks of the microphone-wielding press corps. Instead of being the interviewee, I became the interviewer for E! and *Extra*, and in December 2009 I cohosted the Citrus Bowl with Joey Fatone. I had a great time. Who would ever have thought such a thing?

I know I still need a bit of practice with that kind of camera work—especially reading the teleprompter and making what comes out of my mouth sound natural—but thanks to Drew's encouragement, I know it's just a matter of time. (I have a whole new appreciation for what *Dancing with the Stars* host Tom Bergeron does.) But I've come a long way, and I never could have done it if Drew hadn't worked so hard to help me realize that just by acting natural and being myself, I can tackle even the most intimidating situations.

Emmitt Smith: Respect

Respect: Everyone wants it. Aretha Franklin sang about it. But Emmitt Smith lives it.

I knew that he had the respect of the sporting world, judging from all the excitement around his agreeing to be on the show. The reactions I got when I told people I'd be partnering with him were even further testimony. No one seemed to have anything bad to say about him. "He's the best running back the Dallas Cowboys ever had." "He's a wonderful family man!" "He's using his connections to help urban renewal projects." In short, Emmitt Smith had everything anyone could possibly want in a celebrity. Everything, I worried, but dancing skills.

In my head, I had an image of a huge football player who was going to lumber into the studio on enormous feet and move as though he were just trying to avoid being tackled. I worried that we wouldn't make it even two weeks on the show.

What I discovered, though, was something totally different from what I'd feared. Dancing and sports have a lot in common, after all—more so than I first suspected, anyway: the competitive spirit, the fancy moves, the grace under pressure, and the ego clashing. But even more than that, there is a sense of respect—for your coaches, your teammates, your competitors, your fans, and, even for yourself—that is absolutely essential in becoming a champion. In the season we danced together, Emmitt opened my eyes to the importance of bringing respect to every aspect of my life.

I met Emmitt for the first time when I flew out to Virginia, where he was visiting with his wife's family. Emmitt didn't want to end his family's summer vacation early in order to start working on the show, so, as is often the case with *Dancing with the Stars*, when the celebrity partner isn't in Los Angeles, the professional dancer is flown to wherever the celebrity is living or working at the time.

A three-person crew and I drove to a dance studio in Norfolk, Virginia, to meet with Emmitt. He surprised me from the moment he walked into the studio: he had a slow but confident gait and looked incredibly cool and casual in a loose-fitting pair of slacks and an untucked golf shirt. He cut a far less imposing figure than I'd imagined. In fact, he was only about five inches taller than I, which made us a good partnership, from a purely physical standpoint.

What also surprised me was that he was not an unrefined jock. There was no cockiness about him at all. His smile exuded a warmth and an openness that made me feel at ease with him as soon as we were introduced. He was so gracious and incredibly down-to-earth. It reminded me of how I felt when I first met Drew Lachey—I felt total comfort instead of the intimidation I'd anticipated.

Right away, Emmitt said that he and his wife were impressed with my dancing ability. They were fans of the show, having watched Drew and me win the season two trophy. For all of my excitement about meeting such a well-respected athlete, he reciprocated the enthusiasm. "I'm excited to learn from the best," he said, grinning. "I was coached for many years on the football field, and I respected and trusted what my coaches had to say. So I am looking at you as my coach now. You're the expert. Whatever you say, whatever you want me to do, just tell me. I'm a good listener, and I am here to learn."

I appreciated his positive attitude, but suddenly the easy atmosphere changed for me. I knew that Emmitt's remarks were meant to put me at ease; he just wanted to let me know that he was open to my direction. Unfortunately, though, his gracious compliments made me a bit uncomfortable because I have never been one to take a compliment well.

In all my years of dancing, I've never allowed myself to linger on praise because I always thought I could be better. My dance teachers and coaches never said that a performance routine, or movement, was perfect. They would say, "That's good. Let's try it again." And that is the attitude I've taken in my self-critiques. To this day, no matter how well I perform, I tell myself that I can be better.

I think a lot of young women struggle with taking compliments well. We find it easier to receive—and believe—criticism than a compliment. But that shouldn't be the case. We should learn how to shake off negative comments that are intended to bruise our minds and instead allow ourselves to accept genuine compliments and constructive criticism. Compliments are a form of congratulations, celebrating something special about you. Constructive criticism (for me, at least) shows where there is room for improvement, makes me want to stand up and fight back, and drives me to succeed on the dance floor and in life. The problem is letting the fact that there's room for improvement blind you to what you've already accomplished.

So instead of absorbing and accepting Emmitt's comments graciously, I shook my head in a clear effort to downplay the moment. "Oh, please," I shrugged, trying to move the conversation along. I felt awkward and wanted to put the focus back on him, but I think he noticed my discomfort with compliments and factored that into how he would interact with me in the future.

I had my first lesson on Emmitt's approach to life the same day. I gave him a pair of Latin dance shoes, which have about a one-and-a-half-inch heel on them. I warned him that they might be awkward to walk in, because they are so different from normal street shoes.

"Oh, I think I can handle putting on a pair of shoes," he replied. Then he stood up and started walking on the hardwood floor. With my eyes and the camera's lens trained on him, he took a few steps, then tripped over his own feet and fell. He tried to catch himself with his hands, but gravity won, and there was the great Emmitt Smith, facedown on the floor.

Instead of getting angry with himself for screwing up something so simple, he burst into laughter. He rolled over, hopped to his feet, and started walking again, this time managing to stay upright. But he couldn't stop giggling, then laughing, then bending over, clapping his hands, and just howling. It was so funny to see Emmitt crack up at himself. The more he laughed, the more I laughed; the more I laughed, the more the crew laughed. Finally, we all had to take a break because we just couldn't hold it together.

What an amazing moment! Just by seeing the way Emmitt could laugh at himself while he was trying to learn, he showed me that he was ready to dive in and push to a place far outside his comfort zone as an athlete. Now he was an aspiring dancer and had no qualms about falling flat on his face, literally, and then picking himself up to try again.

That first day was full of surprises. Emmitt did not move the way I thought a football player would move. As we stood side by side in front of the mirrors in the dance studio, I showed him the basic steps of the cha-cha-cha while he mimicked me.

His body was thick and solid, yet his movements were fluid and his footwork was nimble. I was impressed by how flexible he was in spite of having such a compact physique. No doubt he learned to be so light on his feet after all those years of fancy and fast maneuvering around defensive linemen on the football field, but I had no idea it would translate so well to the dance floor.

In the weeks that followed, Emmitt and I talked during the rehearsal breaks, and I really got a chance to learn more about his personality and his outlook on life. I was so struck by his thoughtfulness. He was the celebrity, the one who was supposed to be the interesting one, yet he was curious about my background, my goals, and my overall well-being. He asked me what I wanted to accomplish in my career, whether I had a boyfriend, whether I was close to my family.

As I responded to each question, Emmitt listened intently. He talked to me seriously about the fact that some people might want to take advantage of my success, especially the people I might date. He said that it happened to guys in the NFL all the time. Once someone starts to get a little bit of fame, suddenly everybody wants to be his friend—but many of these "friends" have their own agendas. He stressed to me that I should always make sure that the people in my life didn't inhibit my goals and my dreams.

At first I thought Emmitt was overreacting. I did not consider myself to be famous. Would people really want to glom onto me, a dancer? That didn't seem likely. But Emmitt could see what I didn't: people were making a connection to the show, and I was a big part of that. I think he noticed my drive and ambition to be the best, and he wanted to help me develop that. The more we talked, the more I understood that his concern came from a genuine place, and I was eager to hear more of his wisdom.

I feel so privileged to have had time with Emmitt, getting to experience a side of his personality that he shares only with a small circle. Football fans may always regard him as a dominant force on the football field, but the Emmitt I know is very caring and sensitive.

He also has an unbelievable work ethic. Every week of that season, Emmitt and I commuted from Los Angeles, where *Dancing with the Stars* tapes, to Dallas, where he lives with his family. Initially I found the trip to be exciting and fun, but by our fourth week it had become absolutely exhausting. We would rehearse in Dallas from Wednesday through Saturday, then fly back to Los Angeles, where we'd rehearse Sunday in the show's studio and do the live televised shows Monday and Tuesday. On Wednesday morning, we'd be back on a plane to Dallas. The jet lag turned into a fatigue that wore both of us down and made dance rehearsals a bit more of a chore.

One week, Emmitt and I flew to Dallas on separate flights, and I arrived at the studio before he did. I was so tired that I pulled the hood of my sweatshirt over my head and lay down on the dirty studio dance floor. When Emmitt arrived, he woke me from a deep sleep. I was so disoriented from the constant travel and rehearsing that I didn't know where I was when I opened my eyes.

Yet despite our exhausting schedule, Emmitt was always eager to learn. He did everything I asked him to perfection. When he had to try particularly hard to master something, he'd be drenched in sweat with a little bit of his tongue sticking out of the side of his mouth. That gesture was Emmitt's version of a "do not disturb" sign. When I saw him do that, I knew to leave him alone and let him work out whatever step he was wrestling to master.

The harder Emmitt tried, the better he became. That's an athlete's mentality for you: keep pushing and never give up until you get it right. It made me feel a need to keep raising the bar by devising more complicated choreography. It was exciting and creative for me as a dance instructor, but it was also stressful. With all the travel, we were both feeling worn down. I started to act cranky and found it difficult to be perky or silly for the cameras, even though I wanted to put a positive face on our rehearsals. There were many days I just wanted to get through our practice so that I could go back to the hotel and conk out. I was working harder than I had ever worked, but my heart wasn't in it the way it should have been. I was letting the stress wear me down without stopping to check my attitude.

On a particularly late night at the studio, Emmitt and I were working on our *paso doble* routine. For some reason, he had a lot of trouble with the twist-turn, which is a basic step in the dance. No matter how many times Emmitt tried, he just couldn't get it. We were in our sixth hour of rehearsal, and even the camera crew had packed up for the night. It was just the two of us. We were hot. We were sweaty. We were hungry. All either of us wanted was to get through one clean run of the dance, and then we could call it a night.

"Okay, let's take it from the top," I barked. I raked my hand through my hair in frustration and started the music over for the umpteenth time. Sure enough, we got to the twist-turn and Emmitt messed up.

"Aw, man!" he huffed. He shook his head and pulled up his shirt to wipe the sweat from his forehead. He paced around in a circle. His shoulders slumped. It was clear he was disappointed with himself.

I let out a loud sigh, marched to the boom box, and started the music over. "Let's go again."

We did and, sure enough, he messed up again. This time I didn't even try to hide my frustration.

"You have got to be kidding me!" I snapped at him. "Why is this happening every f———ing time? This is ridiculous!"

I rolled my eyes. I was wound tight, seething, and I clearly didn't hold back. As I stormed over to the music to turn it off, I could feel that Emmitt was focused on me. He paused for a moment, staring intensely and unhappily at my face, then walked calmly across the room to where I was standing.

"Nobody talks to me like that," he said in a very quiet, controlled voice. "Don't think that you're such a special person that you can talk to me like that. None of my football coaches ever spoke to me like that. Do we understand each other?"

"Yes. Yes," I said, looking down. "I'm sorry, Emmitt. I didn't mean to take it out on you. I'm just so frustrated." I couldn't believe that I'd just managed to make our worst night of rehearsal even worse.

"I know. Let's call it a night," he said. The heels of his Latin dance shoes, the same ones that tripped him up the first day we met, echoed off the floor as he walked across the room to gather his things.

It wasn't his size or his strength that intimidated me, it was the way Emmitt spoke to me in a composed and controlled voice. I felt like a daughter who had just disappointed her father. Instead of yelling at me, Emmitt took the approach of being understated and intense. It had a big impact.

I stood silently in the room, but the voice inside my head was chastising me for snapping at him, for releasing my stress in such a highly unproductive and rude way. "Cheryl," I lectured myself, "what is going on here? This guy is not a dance pro! Maybe the problem is you. Maybe you're not teaching him the right way."

That was it. That was exactly the problem. I thought I was disappointed in Emmitt, but in reality the words that I blurted out were an expression of frustration with myself. I was so tired and so stressed out at that point that I wasn't making sense as a teacher to my student, and I took that out on him. The voice in my head—the relentless, driven perfectionist—was berating me over and over for not being able to explain the move in a way that Emmitt could learn. His struggles were my failures, and I was furious with myself for failing. So I took it out on him. I felt so ashamed.

Emmitt put me in my place by confronting me, and I deserved it. He gained my admiration and respect for doing that, and he also caused me to take a good look at myself. I like to think that I am a respectful person, yet I am often harshly critical of myself. That night, back in my hotel room, I thought long and hard about why I disrespected myself like that. Why don't I think better of myself? Why do I even give credence to that demeaning voice in my head?

When I was younger, I was always working to be better. Because I never let myself believe anything was perfect, nothing was ever good enough. There was never a sense of "That's it!" There was never an end to something. My mind was always pushing me toward what was next. How could I do it better? What could I change next time to really nail it? I've been on the receiving end of blunt criticism for so long, both from other people and from my own nagging perfectionism, that sometimes that's just how I communicate. But that night, Emmitt's words made me realize that criticism delivered without respect is only belittling and rude.

Emmitt didn't want to be coddled or patted on the back every time he did something right; he just wanted respect, no matter how the routine turned out. I think he recognized that a sense of respect was something I needed to extend to myself as well. I had to step back and remind myself that I wasn't teaching a fellow dancer. I had to remember to exercise patience instead of flying off the handle and thinking, "Oh, no, he's not getting this step. I'm a terrible teacher. Maybe I better change the whole routine." I needed to take better care of myself so I could be a more responsive instructor. I couldn't push myself to the breaking point in pursuit of a perfection I would never allow myself to see anyway. I needed more sleep, better meals, and a little perspective.

The next day Emmitt got the step right. All he needed was to come at it fresh in the morning. I should have known that. When he nailed it, I was so proud, yet there was still a little pang left over from the night before. I really wished that I hadn't allowed myself to get to that point in order for us to finally master our biggest hurdle thus far. But I shook it off. I was determined not to let that bullying voice disrespect me any more.

We celebrated our little victory by—what else?—doing the routine over again. And again. We may not have been perfect, but I was determined to be happy, for once, with "good enough."

Emmitt and I never talked again about our confrontation, and I think that's because we didn't need to. He had addressed the problem he'd seen, and I had taken action on it. There is no point in dwelling on the past—especially if you are always looking ahead and setting new goals.

I am much more aware now, thanks to Emmitt, that respect is a two-way street. You've got to earn it from others and demand it from yourself. He and I have kept in touch with each other, and when my first studio opened, Emmitt called me to tell me how proud he was. He told me how glad he was to see that the talks we had had years ago had sunk in and how happy he was that I was building a future for myself.

"This is only the beginning for you," he said. But then, because he knows me and how I can be, he added, "But don't forget to enjoy the moment. You've earned it."

Ian Ziering: Think Bigger

Because I had won the mirror ball trophy two seasons in a row—my first two seasons on the show—Ian Ziering was a bit giddy when he learned that we were going to be partners.

"We're going to win!" he squealed when he walked into the studio for our first meeting.

"No pressure!" I laughed.

One day, after rehearsal, Ian and I went to get coffee near the dance studio where we were practicing. We were talking about life and careers, and he asked me, "So what do you want to do with your career after this? You have won the show twice already, and you're a huge success. The audience really responds to you."

"They respond to the show," I said.

"Well, yeah, they do. But you should create a brand for yourself. Franchise and create your own studios."

"I have thought about having a dance studio of my own," I said. "I don't know about a franchise, though."

"You could have franchises all over the country. The time to capitalize on all of this is now."

I was flattered by the confidence he had in me, but I didn't really believe that this could ever happen, because I had some real insecurities and I didn't realize just how highly people regarded my talents as a dancer. In addition, I didn't think I'd ever have the time to make it all happen. I was just enjoying living in the moment, and I hadn't thought broadly about my future or about building on the success I'd achieved on *Dancing with the Stars*. It was still kind of new for me.

That afternoon Ian and I discussed what my future could hold. He had a lot of ideas for me—and I did a good job shooting each of them down. But by the end of our chat, he had built up my confidence enough that I realized maybe some of his ideas weren't so far-fetched after all.

It made perfect sense that Ian was telling me to think bigger about my career. When he got his big break, he was on a little show called *Beverly Hills, 90210*. It started small, then found a loyal audience and took off. Ian knew that a small seed is all you need to make something grow. He made me open my eyes to being proactive about branding myself. I thought it was the most stupid, egotistical thing to name a studio after myself, but Ian reassured me that it wasn't. "That's what branding is!" he insisted. "You are the face of dance on television. When people hear 'Cheryl Burke,' they think 'great dancer.'"

When I got home that day I talked to my mom about it. She and I had previously tossed around the idea of having a studio, but we hadn't really put anything into motion. When she heard the motivation in my voice, she started researching how we could go about opening a studio.

Had it not been for Ian, I don't know that I would have been aggressive enough about furthering my career. He helped me to visualize taking my dance career to a level where I really could connect with people on an individual basis.

My mom found our first studio location in Potrero Hill and began the process of converting it from a dream to an actual dance studio. In April 2008, we opened the first Cheryl Burke Dance studio and since then, we've opened up two more studios: one in Mountain View, California, and one in Laguna Niguel, California. More are on the way, because we have partnered with a franchise company to expand across the nation. It's all thanks to Ian, who urged me to realize that it was possible.

Wayne Newton: Always Take Time for Others

Of all my partners, the one I keep in regular touch with most is Wayne Newton. I was privileged enough to form a connection with Wayne that was strong and genuine. He does not have a bad bone in his body, which is one of the main reasons he is a living legend. He is kind, humble, and so appreciative of everything that has happened in his life that it's impossible not to love him.

When Wayne and I began rehearsing together the summer before the season five premiere, he was finishing up a tour. I accompanied him everywhere he went so that we could keep up our practice schedule. He had a vacation to Hawaii planned with his entire family. He insisted that I come along as well, and he extended an invitation to my boyfriend at the time to come along, too. It was beyond generous. Wayne got us a beautiful suite at the same hotel where he was staying, and he kept checking in with me to make sure I was okay.

"Are you having a good time? Is there anything I can do for you?" he asked over and over. It was so thoughtful, so over-the-top nice that I figured it couldn't be genuine. He just seemed too good to be true. But now I understand that being kind-hearted and generous is just who Wayne Newton is. I consider it a privilege to call him my friend.

When we went on the *Dancing with the Stars* tour in the winter of 2007–2008, there were at least a hundred cast and crew who traveled with the production. Wayne knew every-one's name—every single person! He talked to everybody and thanked them after every performance, no matter what. He made that a priority, because he knew, as a performer himself, that he could not do what he does best without every person behind the scenes giving his or her best effort.

Wayne is the ultimate gentleman. He taught me to be kind to everyone I work with, no matter what the person's job is or how difficult people make it to get along with them. There are many different personalities in this world, and the best way to deal with them is to be kind and considerate and to always leave the room with a smile on your face. Wayne's philosophy is that people hold on to that pleasantness more than anything else.

When I was being scrutinized and criticized by the press for gaining weight in the fall of 2008, Wayne was the rock I leaned on. He was so supportive. I wanted to lash out at anyone and everyone because I was so angry and hurt by it all. I took the bloggers' criticism and negative comments personally, and I had a hard time maintaining a positive attitude. I talked to Wayne about it on the phone one day, and he gave me some good advice.

"Cheryl, don't let anyone see that you are hurting. This kind of thing happens to entertainers all the time. People will try to bash you, and it's important that you keep your head held high. Don't let anyone see your weakness outside your home. When you're out in public, people will be watching you, and you need to put a smile on your face at all times."

Wayne has been ridiculed in the press for different things throughout his career, yet he still manages to keep a smile on his face. He told me that he's able to stay positive about life and the entertainment industry because it has brought him such joy. He told me that he is grateful for every experience he has had—good and bad—because it's gotten him to where he is today. He doesn't dwell on the negative; he hangs on to the many positive things in his life: his family, his friends, and his career. Now that's the kind of attitude I try to have as well, and one of those positive things is Wayne's presence as a mentor in my life.

Cristian de la Fuente: Loyalty

At the time I was dancing with Cristian de la Fuente, a tabloid article came out that Drew Lachey and I were having an affair. It was an awful thing to see in print, and what made it worse was that a lot of other press outlets started picking up the report as well.

Cristian could see that I was upset by the horrible accusation being splashed on the cover of *Star*. We both were living in the same apartment building, near the *Dancing with the Stars* studio, so we often rode to and from rehearsals together.

The day the magazine came out, he picked me up and, being the gentleman that he is, he drove around Los Angeles to buy every copy of the magazine in order to take it off the newsstands.

He hardly knew me at that point. We had been dance partners for only about six weeks. But he instantly showed me how loyal a friend he was by doing that. He said that he didn't want me, my friends, or my family to have to go into any store and see that article on the rack.

I couldn't believe what a huge gesture he made for me, but he said, "You are my friend, and when I call someone my friend, I take care of them. I will always be your friend."

He also thanked me for taking care of him and helping him to look his best on television. I was teaching him to dance on the show, which ended up being a big boost to his popularity. Cristian had a very successful career as an actor in Mexico and Central and South America, but he wasn't really discovered by audiences in the United States until he appeared on *Dancing with the Stars*.

We jokingly made a bet that if I could teach him to dance well enough to reach the finals, he'd take me and four of my friends to his native Chile. Cristian kept his end of the bargain, which was to give his all to dancing and to be the best competitor he could be. I, as his dance instructor, choreographed to the best of my abilities, accentuating his strengths as a performer. Much to our delight, we made it to the finale—even with Cristian suffering an injury to his left bicep the week before the semifinals.

After the finale, Cristian, his publicist, and a few friends got together for an informal dinner at the Grove in Los Angeles. As we sat at the table, Cristian raised a glass and said, "I have to hand it to you, my friend. You did it. You're going to Chile to visit with me and my family." And he meant it!

A few months later, when a group of us had a break from work, we made the trip. Cristian put us up at the luxurious Ritz Hotel in Santiago. It was a first-class experience all the way. We went skiing, did some wine tasting, and indulged in great meals at night. It had really just started as a joke, but Cristian was determined to follow through. He is truly a man of his word, and he is one of the most loyal friends I have in my life today.

Maurice Greene: Laughter Is the Best Medicine

When I was partnered with one of the most celebrated U.S. Olympic athletes for season seven, I knew it was going to be great.

I felt that way from the start, because Maurice Greene, a track and field superstar, had so much positive energy. After a few days of rehearsals together, I finally asked him, "Are you always this way?"

He bounced up and down with a big smile. "Yes, ma'am, I am!" The amount of enthusiasm he had was unreal.

The first week we were on the dance floor for the season premiere, the tabloids and the Internet bloggers targeted me for putting on weight. I was already self-conscious, and the mean-spirited comments in magazines and online made me want to crawl into a hole.

Maurice really helped me to take a step back and find the humor in it all. He had quite a knack of finding the lighter side of things in life. He and I never talked about the weight issue, but he could see that it was upsetting to me, and in his own special way he boosted my spirits by being his upbeat personable self. He always greeted me with a hug and an awesome smile.

When we met for rehearsal, he greeted me with, "Hey, sexy lady!" He always commented on how graceful I looked when I demonstrated a move. I wore a sweat suit during rehearsals, with my hair pulled back in a ponytail and no makeup on, yet he told me how great I looked. On show nights we met before heading to the soundstage, and he always said, "Wow, you look great" or "You look like a million bucks tonight!"

His compliments were very uplifting and exactly what I needed at the time. No matter what kind of negativity was outside the dance studio, once we were inside, it was all about having fun. Sometimes Maurice sang, and sometimes he burst out in a dance that he said he wanted to try at a club. It always made me laugh, and it took my mind off the pettiness that had put me in a bad mood.

Press interviews that season were not easy for me. I felt so uncomfortable in front of the cameras because of the whole weight issue, and everybody seemed to want to ask me how I felt about it. One night, after a performance show, Maurice and I were making the media rounds, and I was obviously down. Maurice surprised me, though. He was always bursting into little rhymes when we were in rehearsals, so when the interviewer asked us how we felt about our performance that night, Maurice burst into laughter. "Winner, winner—chicken dinner!" he belted out.

I cracked up. So did the camera guy and the interviewer. No one—not even Maurice, I think—had any idea what that meant. But it deflected attention from me and made us all laugh hysterically, which was exactly what I needed. It also became our little mantra of sorts for the rest of our time on the show. Every time we finished a routine, we said, "Winner, winner—chicken dinner!" to each other.

I guess it just goes to show you that not everything makes sense in life. And when that happens, you have to smile and say something completely illogical just to make yourself laugh.

Gilles Marini: Enjoy Life to Its Fullest

Although Gilles Marini is regarded as a sex god by women around the world, he really isn't one to me. In my opinion, what makes Gilles amazing isn't his gorgeous physical appearance, it's what he's got on the inside. The man is made of substance and goodness.

When you are in a room with Gilles, he makes you feel like the most important person in the world. I've seen him do that with his three-year-old daughter, with his wife, and with fans who stop him on the street to take a picture. Lord knows, he did that with me.

He talks to everyone, no matter who they are. When he came to the opening of my third studio in Laguna Niguel in May 2009, he didn't just take a picture at the ribbon-cutting ceremony, shake a couple of hands, or sign a few autographs. Gilles was out on the dance floor dancing with everybody all night long. It was a magical night for me and my fans, who just ate up Gilles's fantastic charisma and personality.

"Live life to the fullest," he told me. "You need to enjoy life more. You're so young, Cheryl. Jump in, and whatever happens, happens!"

Ask yourself: Am I doing this because I love it or because it will please somebody else?

I thought all along that that was what I was already doing. But I wasn't. I often second-guessed myself, or I'd do something because it was easy rather than tackle a challenge; or because I'd always done something, I automatically thought I had to keep doing it. Gilles made me understand that it's okay to buck the trend and step outside my comfort zone from time to time.

Gilles had so much confidence in me. I never gave myself credit for putting together good routines for us to perform on the show. I was stressed out every week about whether our routines were good enough, but Gilles kept on reassuring me that my work was amazing and that I should stop questioning my abilities; I should believe wholeheartedly in myself and my talents. Gilles also motivated me to go out on stage and entertain to my fullest potential every time. He gave his all and made me want to try harder.

Gilles does things in life because he wants to do them, not because he feels obligated to do them. He is a family man, and he would do anything for his wife and his kids, but he's also all about grabbing life by the horns. He takes risks and has experiences that he relishes, for better or worse. Doing the naked scene in the *Sex and the City* movie was a risky venture. When he landed on *Dancing with the Stars*, nobody really knew who he was beyond that, but he dove in and gave it all that he had. Now he's a very in-demand actor for television projects, because people went wild for his charming personality and his work ethic. He's also adored by his fans and travels the world to make personal appearances. He enjoys every moment, and he helped me to make sure that I enjoy mine.

Thanks to the encouragement Gilles gave me, I now have a better sense of confidence. He helped me learn to take pride in my work, to never doubt myself, and to love where I am. Those are all very valuable lessons, indeed.

Tom DeLay: It's Okay to Agree to Disagree

There was a lot of media hype over former house of Representatives majority leader Tom DeLay joining the season nine cast. There were press reports that he was an evil person, all based on his colorful political career. All the hype affected my perception of him when I found out that he was my partner, but it was short-lived. It's certainly true that the man has his opinions, but so does everyone. That's what life is about. A lot of people hide their thoughts, but Tom chooses not to, and I think that's great.

I've gotten to see that Tom DeLay the politician and Tom DeLay the private person are two different people. Tom DeLay the person is a sweet man who is deeply in love with his wife and who is a devoted father to his daughter. He's also a silly dog person who gets on the floor to play with his two beloved bichon frises, Bailey and Taylor.

Tom has lived through so many different experiences, and he has a lot to say. I had so many interesting conversations with him, but not one of them ever touched on politics. I knew that my views might not be in line with his beliefs, and I think he knew that about me, too. Still, we were able to connect as human beings who love people and life.

I think that because Tom has a daughter who is not much older than I am, he felt a bit paternal toward me. He was so curious about my career and my life and how I got to where I am now. He asked me all sorts of questions and really wanted to learn about me. I asked him about his life and how he enjoyed living in Washington and Texas. He had so many great stories about working in the nation's capital, meeting dignitaries and world leaders, which I found to be fascinating because his life was so foreign to my own experiences. It occurred to me that what I do is so vastly different from anything Tom has ever done in his life. We could both learn from each other.

My time with Tom taught me that although our views in life may differ, our passion for life and people is very similar. I never in a million years thought I'd find common ground with a conservative politician who is forty years my senior, but it was great to share so much time with someone whom I consider an intriguing man and a quality human being.

Chad Ochocinco: What You See Isn't Always What You Get

The football players who have danced on our show in the past—guys like Jerry Rice, Emmitt Smith, Jason Taylor, and Warren Sapp—had a pretty good track record for going far in the competition. So I was hopeful when I heard that I was going to be paired with Cincinnati Bengals star Chad Ochocinco for season ten.

As I do every season, I immediately went to my computer and Googled my new partner's name. I read all about Chad's outspoken and downright cocky personality. Chad is a star on the football field, and he knows it. He also thrives on fan attention. I watched YouTube videos of him in which he showboated for the crowd; when he scored a touchdown, he did an entertaining victory dance or jumped into the stands to get some love from his fans. When he disagreed with a referee's call, he didn't hesitate to loudly voice his opinion. He was so over-the-top that I started to think that this might be the most interesting season yet.

My shyness from way back in season two had left me long ago, so I wasn't afraid to meet my new partner, even one whose reputation was bigger than life. I imagined that when Chad walked in the door, I was probably not going to have to say much at all. I could let him chat and quip and mug for the camera crew while I just went along for the ride, and the photographers would get all the footage they needed from him.

But when Chad walked into the room the first day, nothing came out of his mouth. He was so reserved that I wondered if someone had spoken to him and said, "Now look—this is a family television show. Just shut up and listen."

No, the producers assured me, they had not said a word at all. In fact, they were counting on Chad's personality to drive our partnership and be great entertainment for the show.

Instead, on the first day, Chad was very quiet. During a break I told him that I had expected him to be a bit more talkative. He smiled—he has the greatest smile in the world—and acknowledged that he was nervous to be doing the show.

"I really want to do my best, and I want you to be hard on me," he said, kind of shuffling, almost as though he were shy. "I want you to tell me the truth, because that's the only way I will get better. I know what you can do with people, and I hope I don't disappoint you."

"There's no way you can ever disappoint me as long as you show up and try your best," I assured him. "Don't put pressure on yourself to instantly be an amazing ballroom dancer. Remember, dancing is supposed to be fun."

He smiled, but I could tell that in the back of his mind he was thinking about what his teammates would say if he didn't do well. He was worried about impressing his kids and showing them that their daddy could do anything. I could see—even though most of the time in those early days together he was very quiet—that he was actually a sweet and kind person who was taking the show very seriously.

In the weeks that followed, I picked up on something interesting. Chad seemed cautious with new people. It was nothing major, but when someone new, like a producer or a press member, walked into a rehearsal, Chad suddenly became very quiet and let me do all the talking. When he was asked a direct question, he responded kindly and softly—the exact opposite of what people were expecting from him. A humble, vulnerable side of his personality came out, and it was surprisingly sweet and genuine.

But the wild side of Chad Ochocinco came out when we moved our training to Miami, where he lives when he's not playing ball in Cincinnati. It was late winter, a couple of weeks after the end of the football season. Miami must be one of the most fun places on earth. It's such a lively city, with a great beach scene, great hotels, and great restaurants. As a single girl, I was happy to be somewhere I could have some fun and unwind after work.

Chad was all about showing me his town. The shy Chad who was sheepishly getting familiar with me in rehearsals was nowhere to be seen. Miami Chad is a guy in his element. He knows the town. He loves the town. And it loves him back.

One of the first days we were there, we went to lunch, and people were hollering his name as they drove by. The attention was something I certainly wasn't used to. People say hello to me in stores and restaurants, but I have never had fans yelling out of their car windows at me.

All the attention made it really hard to blend in—but I learned quickly that blending in isn't something that Chad does very well. Judging from his cars, he isn't really trying to, either. Chad drives a screaming orange Lamborghini, a "look at me" baby blue Hummer, and a one-of-a-kind tow truck that I had to climb up on to get into the passenger seat.

Because Chad is so good-looking and fun and single, people assumed that we'd be a perfect match—and not just on the dance floor. We had been working together only a couple of weeks when my publicist, Susan, got calls asking if Chad and I were an item. The rumor mill was getting fired up—and this time, with due cause.

Chad and I had a great time that couple of weeks in Miami, and in between the flash and flair of his public celebrity persona, we had some great talks about family and career. He came from a very poor background, surrounded by crime and drugs. Despite the odds being against him, he found that his athletic talent could pull him and his family out of that existence and afford them the finer things in life. Chad was very proud of his accomplishments, as he should be. He came from nothing, worked hard, and made something of himself. I admired him for that. But I also saw that at times Chad thought money could conquer all.

We developed a nice friendship in the early weeks of the show, and Chad continually wanted to show me how much he appreciated my teaching by giving me gifts like fancy jewelry. The third week of the season, after the live shows had begun, Chad gave me a huge diamond ring. It was gorgeous, but I thought it was far too fancy for me to accept. He insisted, however.

I was flattered by his thoughtfulness and his generosity, but I had to explain to him that I had my own money and could buy jewelry anytime I wanted. What mattered to me was how he treated me. He was always kind, but I knew I would never be the only girl in his life.

"Material things don't feed my soul," I explained to him. "What happens if we start dating and I get attached to you—and then you have other women you want to see?"

He respected where I was coming from, but he wasn't used to a woman not falling all over herself to date him. Although Chad was wooing me, I had to resist because, ultimately, he doesn't believe in relationships. As much as I liked him, I couldn't let myself fall for him, because I knew that there would always be somebody else. I know that the girl I used to be would be okay with seeing this kind of guy, taking whatever attention and time he was willing to offer, but the woman I am now needs, wants, and deserves more. I'm not going to sit on the sidelines and wait my turn.

All of this was going on during season ten while I was teaching Chad how to dance; it made for an interesting mix. There were times we had a blast in rehearsals and laughed our heads off, then there were times we were barely speaking. It was a roller-coaster ride of sorts, mostly because throughout the whole ordeal, Chad was frustrated that the dancing was harder than he had ever imagined it would be.

The judges' comments every week were harsh and really did a number on Chad's confidence. It was frustrating for me, because I knew how hard he worked in rehearsals. But our scores were so low. The first six weeks of the season, it was his fans and Twitter followers who kept him on the show.

"I feel like I'm letting you down," Chad confessed in rehearsal one day. "I had no idea this was going to be so hard."

I tried to reassure him that he needed to think of it like a bad game on the football field. I was his coach and had to make sure that he knew I wasn't giving up on him.

"You need to get out of your head and focus on what lies ahead, not what happened yesterday," I told him. "We are here for whatever reasons brought us here. So what if the judges have been tough? We have a new dance and a clean slate when we walk into the ballroom next Monday. So forget about what's done and be confident you will do well going forward."

"I can't be confident with something I just don't do. This is so not my world," he said.

"You have to trust me that this is your world right now and you belong, because I believe in you and your fans believe in you," I insisted.

He smiled his incredible smile and we rehearsed the Viennese waltz again, a very lovely and special dance. Fellow *Dancing* pro Tony Dovolani came to one of our rehearsals that week to give Chad some tips he could relate to.

"You need to extend your arms, like the ball is being thrown out here," Tony said, reaching his right arm into the air, "and not at the numbers on your jersey."

Tony kept inserting football metaphors into his pep talk with Chad, and I could see that all of a sudden Chad was making a breakthrough. He got into the romance and the flirtation of the dance and seemed to let go of his inhibitions.

We performed the Viennese waltz on May 3, 2010, a day I'll not soon forget, because it was also my birthday and I received two very special gifts. The first was a beautiful crystal and diamond necklace that Chad gave me that day. It was lovely. He also filled my trailer with balloons and flowers.

But the other gift, the best one of all, was one that money couldn't buy: Chad's performance. Chad and I did our dance that night, and we received not only a standing ovation from the audience but also incredibly kind comments from the judges.

"There is nothing sexier than watching a man find out how to be tender and graceful," Carrie Ann gushed.

"Remember this date," Len said. "The night you became a contender."

The audience squealed, and Chad and I hugged tightly. But the best was yet to come: our scores. We received twenty-eight points out of a possible thirty, which was the highest score we'd received all season. I was bowled over. Chad was speechless. Getting those comments and that score from the judges did wonders for his self-confidence. It was concrete validation for all of the hard work he had been putting in week after week.

It was certainly a night and a season to remember. Chad and I made it to the top four couples and were eliminated from the competition just one week before the finals. Even though we didn't win the mirror ball trophy, we both felt victorious. I felt like a winner because I was able to teach my student to have confidence in his abilities. And Chad felt like a winner because he went from absolutely no ballroom dancing ability to being a bona fide contender in the season.

What became of us off the dance floor? Well, I can tell you that I will always have a soft spot for Chad in my heart, and I know that he feels the same way about me. As the saying goes, what you see isn't always what you get. He was not the guy I imagined he would be: headstrong, self-assured, obnoxious. And I don't think that I was like any of the girls he was used to being around. I had opinions and ambitions and dreams of my own. I didn't need him to take care of me, and I didn't throw myself at him.

I found myself drawn to this sweet, kindhearted man, and he found himself drawn to my self-awareness and independence. One thing I know for sure is that we earned each other's trust and respect, and I am certain we will always be friends.

Rick Fox: Enjoy the Journey

For my tenth season on the show I was partnered with Rick Fox, three-time NBA champion forward for the Los Angeles Lakers. Based on my past experiences with athletes, I was certain that Rick would have a great work ethic and a focused, disciplined mind-set when it came rehearsals. I also looked at his lean physique and incredibly tall six-foot seven-inch stature. As a player, Rick was able to move nimbly about the basketball court, swiftly gliding along the parquet floor while he dribbled the ball from one end to the other. He can do two things at once, I thought. This will be good!

I started to choreograph our first dance, the waltz. Rick and I talked about the dance, the movements, the posture required. We went through the initial steps of the dance for a while and, unlike some partners I've had in the past, during that first run-through of the dance, Rick was calm. Unusually calm. I remarked to him that I was glad to see that he wasn't freaked out by trying to dance, and he told me that he was going to be open to whatever the experience brought his way.

I was struck by what he said. He went on to tell me that in his younger days he focused on working hard and getting results. "Put in the time and get the prize at the end of the rainbow" seemed to be the unofficial motto of his life growing up. I could relate to that. The harder I worked as a dancer, the more competitions I wanted to win. Practice, compete, win; it was the natural progression of things in my mind.

"Yes, that's how it was when I was younger," Rick told me. "But I've learned that along the way, it's the journey where you really learn the most—the obstacles you face, the defeats you suffer, the injuries you overcome—that truly teach you the most about life."

For years, I have been focused on my goals and the work required to achieve them. Once I reach one, I set my sights on the next goal. I have been like a task master with my career, working to have an alternate plan in place so that when the time comes when I don't dance every day, my plan B will be there to buoy me along.

"You can't always have a plan B," Rick told me. "You need to be open to things in life and let the universe kind of present different options, different choices to you. Many times the best opportunities and experiences in life are the ones you least expect."

Sure, we talked about work while we rehearsed our waltz, but we also talked a great deal about our growth as people, which, for me, included relationships. I'm single, and I'm not sure I want to be that anymore. I want to meet people and date again.

"It's not that people aren't interested in dating you," Rick said. "You need to ask yourself if you are ready to date. If you're not giving off the energy that you're ready and open, then people won't pick that up. It doesn't matter so much what you say, it's what you feel and how you communicate that. Maybe you're not ready to have a new man come into your life because you're focusing on so many other things."

Rick hit the nail on the head. He encouraged me to reflect on the fact that maybe I'm thinking too much about tomorrow and not enjoying what's happening today. "Enjoy the journey and embrace life's ups and downs," he advised me.

During our partnership I was the dance coach and Rick was my life coach. I fondly referred to him as my "gentle giant." He was there for me, like an unexpected gift from the universe—the very kind he told me to watch for.

Sure, we would focus primarily on our dance, but he also made sure to ask about where my head was at and how things were with me personally. The more we talked about ourselves rather than focusing strictly on the dance, the more my stress level was reduced.

Generally speaking, on the days of the live shows I'm a bundle of nerves. Season after season I paced and worried as I reviewed each dance in my head. I often second-guessed whether my partner and I were ready to perform, obsessing over every small detail that might trip us up even slightly. But on the day of the first live show with Rick, I was incredibly calm—because he was so calm. I asked him how he was feeling. He smiled his incredible smile and remarked, "I feel great—well-coached and prepared!" He said he could feel the positive energy that was in the air.

His words, his smile, his attitude were all calming. I felt myself "get out of my head," as Rick often advised me, and I started just enjoying the night, too. For the first time ever I wasn't concerned with how far my partner and I would go on the show. Instead, I was more excited to sit back and enjoy the journey.

Thanks, Again

I want to express my gratitude to the men who have been more than just dance partners to me. Long after the cheers of the crowd faded and long after our seasons ended, I have held on to what these men taught me, and they have made me grateful for all of life's blessings. I am truly blessed to do what I do, to live where I live, and to have such wonderful family and friends in my life. These men gave me encouragement when I felt weak and vulnerable. They reinforced my belief that hard work does pay off and that I should never compromise. They taught me to dream bigger and to never forget who I am. Each, in his own way, helped to make me the stronger and more confident person I am today, and for that I will always be grateful.

AFTERWORD

I've chosen the dances highlighted in this book as the ones to share, but there are so many other dances I've done on the show and in my life that have been significant for me. My hope is that in the years to come I will continue to grow as a dancer and choreographer and, most of all, as a human being.

I love that there are so many different types of dance shows out there now. *Dancing with the Stars* kicked things off, and now there is so much programming, like *So You Think You Can Dance*, *America's Best Dance Crew*, *Dance Your Ass Off*, and *America's Got Talent*. It's exciting to see that dancing is being recognized as an art form and as a sport. I don't think that many people outside the dance world have ever really appreciated what it takes to be a dancer. Ten years ago, dancers were the backup people. We were faceless and nameless. Now people are getting to know dancers' personalities and strengths. They respect and appreciate what we do artistically and athletically, and it feels great to be part of a big dance resurgence.

As my career continues to grow, there are going to be many more stories in my life than the few I've shared here. But it has been exciting and gratifying to have the opportunity to share what I have written here about my childhood, my entrée into dance, and my life as a professional dancer and choreographer, a businesswoman, and an adult living in Los Angeles. I have so much to say, and I have learned over the years that my career gives me a unique opportunity to reach out to people to share my struggles and triumphs and, I hope, help someone else in the process.

I have been blessed with some incredible fans who reach out to me by e-mail or who stop me in airports or when I'm running errands around town. They tell me that I've influenced them in so many different ways. Some of them want to learn how to dance, some of them tell me I've made them want to take steps toward leading a healthier life, and others tell me that I've been a role model for their young daughters.

They tell me that I've changed their lives. But they've also changed my life. I've learned to live the life I want to live despite being in the spotlight. There is a part of me that has grown tremendously by being on one of the most popular television shows in the country. I feel a responsibility to be as honest and as open as I can with my fans, because that's how they have been with me.

I am very conscious of making sure that I send the right message about body image. Be proud of the individual you are and don't let anyone convince you that you aren't worth celebrating.

I shared the trauma of being molested as a child because I wanted other victims to know that it's okay to feel sad and angry and confused. It's not easy, nor is healing an overnight process. But I want people to know that it is possible to move beyond those feelings and begin to win back your life from those memories. I'm living proof of that. This book, being able to tell my story to everybody, has made me a stronger person. It has made me grow as a person. The *paso doble* chapter was certainly the scariest one for me to write, but it was cathartic to chronicle that experience, to put it down on paper, and to know that now, two decades later, those experiences do not define me.

I'd like to share one final story that I think best illustrates what my career as a dancer has taught me.

It was after my first season on the show, when I danced with Drew Lachey. I got a phone call from my publicist, Susan, early one morning while I was visiting with my dance coach in New York City. "Cheryl," Susan said, her voice serious but excited. "You got nominated for two Emmys this morning."

I was dumbfounded. "What do you mean? The Emmys? What are you talking about?" I asked.

"This is a huge deal," she said, beaming. "The show's producers put your work forward for consideration, and your choreography was recognized by the Academy. I'm so happy for you. You should be very proud of yourself."

I was speechless. I had just started in the business, yet my work was being recognized next to some of the most celebrated living figures in the dance world. I could barely process it all.

I called my mom, and she was so proud. "I always knew that if people could see you dance, they would sit up and take notice," she said, her voice cracking as she tried to contain her tears of happiness. All of those years of dance lessons, all of those weekend dance competitions and flying around the globe, had led up to this incredible moment.

I took my mom to the Emmy awards show with me. We got dressed up and walked down the red carpet. It was one of the greatest nights of my life. After living in Los Angeles for nearly nine months, I had walked down a good many red carpets at big events, but nothing topped the long walk my mom and I made as reporters asked me how it felt to be nominated.

In a word, it felt amazing. It felt even more meaningful to share that night with my mom, who never failed to encourage me and push me to pursue dancing. She realized before I did that it was a passion for me. She told me that I come alive on the dance floor.

I did not win the Emmy. I was up against one of the most amazing choreographers of all time, Kenny Ortega. He had worked on a little television movie called *High School Musical* that absolutely swept the nation. Kenny took home the beautiful Emmy statue that night for outstanding choreography—as well he should have. A few reporters asked me afterward if I was disappointed that I didn't win. Are you kidding me? No way. Just having my name listed in the program alongside Kenny Ortega's was something I could barely wrap my mind around. It's a cliché, I know, but it truly is an honor just to be nominated.

What I took away from that night was that as a dancer and a choreographer, I am exactly where I belong. And ultimately, that is the lesson for all of us. We each need to find the thing that we were born to do; we need to allow ourselves to become the person we were meant to be.

Your passions, your talents, and your personal story are all part of who you are. I have been fortunate enough to have an incredible family and group of friends around me as I have fought through minor setbacks as well as some major challenges in my quest to develop my potential. That is what I consider to be my greatest accomplishment. It has nothing to do with Emmy statues or mirror ball trophies, as great as those things are. In the end, the greatest victory we can know is the result of all of our hard work, discipline, and dedication: the realization of our dreams.